Stories for telling

35 Bible-based narratives for all ages

kevin mayhew

First published in 2004 by
KEVIN MAYHEW LTD
Buxhall, Stowmarket, Suffolk, IP14 3BW
E-mail: info@kevinmayhewltd.com

KINGSGATE PUBLISHING INC
1000 Pannell Street, Suite G, Columbia, MO 65201
E-mail: sales@kingsgatepublishing.com

© 2004 Michael Forster

The right of Michael Forster to be identified as the author of this work has been asserted by him in accordance with the Copyright, Designs and Patents Act 1988.

All rights reserved. No part of this publication may be reproduced, stored in a retrieval system, or transmitted, in any form or by any means, electronic, mechanical, photocopying, recording or otherwise, without the prior written permission of the publisher.

9 8 7 6 5 4 3 2 1 0
ISBN 1 84417 212 0
Catalogue No. 1500688

Cover design by Angela Selfe
Edited by Katherine Laidler
Typesetting by Louise Selfe
Printed and bound in Great Britain

Contents

Foreword	5
Let's get creative *Genesis 1:1-2:3*	7
We'll do it our way *Genesis 3*	12
Remember the rainbow *Genesis 6-9*	17
Towering ambition *Genesis 11:1-9*	21
In your dreams, Jacob! *Genesis 28:11-22*	25
Moses in the rushes *Exodus 2:1-10*	29
A burning desire for freedom *Exodus 3:1-15*	33
Just walk this way *Exodus 14:5-31*	37
God feeds his people *Exodus 16:2-25*	42
Now, take it easy, God! *Exodus 32:1-24*	46
He's the greatest – honest! *1 Samuel 16:1-13*	50
Power tends to corrupt *2 Samuel 11:1-27*	54
The game's up, David *2 Samuel 11:26-12:13a*	58
Elijah and the widow *1 Kings 17:1-16*	62
You're never alone *1 Kings 19:9-18*	66
The God-given right to do wrong? *1 Kings 21:1-24*	70
Oh, just do it! *2 Kings 5:1-14*	74
New life for old bones *Ezekiel 37:1-14*	78
You can run but you can't hide *Jonah 1-2*	82
God shows who really counts *Luke 2:1-20*	87
The King, the Pretender and the Three Wise Guys *Matthew 2:1-12*	91
Do it my way *Matthew 4:1-11*	95
Don't panic! *Mark 5:21-43*	99
Holy wasteful *Matthew 13:1-9*	103
God's not fair – he's generous *Matthew 20:1-16*	106
Disabled access upstairs *Mark 2:1-12*	110

Who's in and who's out? *Mark 7:24-30*	114
Who does he think he is? *Luke 4:14-30*	117
I know I'm forgiven *Luke 7:36-50*	122
What do you mean, 'Neighbour'? *Luke 10:25-37*	127
A fool and his money *Luke 12:13-21*	131
Jesus confronts Jerusalem *Luke 19:28-48*	134
A passion for people *Luke 23:1-49*	139
They think it's all over *Luke 24:1-12*	144
Don't just sit there – communicate *Acts 2:1-11*	148

Foreword

Picture the scene: the people's faces glow in the light of the campfire. The children's eyes are bright as they listen to tales of the Olden Days, told by One Who Was There. The adults round the campfire eagerly relish the re-telling of the stories – *their* stories – for this is *their* history, and they love it. The tension rises as some great peril is again recalled from the safe confines of memory to loom again like a great shadow over the company. Then – relief as the climax of the tale is reached and the saving power of God can be celebrated. The tension is released in laughter and songs of praise.

Now, does that sound like something we'd all like to have been part of? Some of us, I guess, have experienced it to greater or lesser extents as our parents or grandparents told us about their experiences of air raids, for example. Although born after the Second World War, I can still 'hear' the wail of the air-raid siren; I can 'feel' the tension of the hurried exodus to the air-raid shelter; I can 'hear' the sighs of relief from my parents on returning to find the house still there, woven into their cries for the neighbours and friends they lost. All of that's very vivid to me, even though I wasn't there, because the stories were told to me in such a way as to make them 'my' stories.

We might have moved into the computer age, but I know from experience that children and adults alike still love a good story, well told, by a real live human being, with plenty of eye contact. I'm also utterly convinced that if we could make that the model for our church life we should stand a chance of engaging children's (not to mention adults') hearts, minds and souls with the faith in effective and lasting ways.

The scene I depicted at the beginning of all this would probably be a fair representation of a regular worship experience for the early (and not so early) Israelites. The relationships that the storytellers built up with their hearers bound them into the community's relationship with God, and the context became part of the story, which became *everybody's* story. I fear that we've lost a lot of that in our determination to 'educate' children and fill them with 'essential' information.

And yet we have many opportunities to recreate this powerful scene in our churches, whether in weekly worship, mid-week activities, celebration meals on special occasions, youth weekends, or whatever. The stories in this book are designed to help with that. The different paragraph styles should give the 'teller' confidence to take their eyes off the script and really engage the audience, knowing they can easily find their place again and continue. Ideally, if preparation time permits, the stories can be learned in advance and told using just the 'crib sheet', allowing more scope for spontaneity and for the personality of the speaker to come through.

How about setting the scene – making it a real campfire or candlelit meal table setting? Why not dress up in period costume? Maybe you should hand this book over to the youth group and ask them to organise a special Church Anniversary dinner or a bonfire night with a difference? Another possibility would be to organise an event on 31 October when celebrating the lives of the great biblical characters could offer a creative alternative to the secular mockery of Hallowe'en. Those are just a few of the ways in which this storytelling material might be used. Now, it's over to you.

Here are the basic ingredients.

Add imagination, and stir well.

Michael Forster

Let's get creative

Based on Genesis 1:1-2:3

Tell me about things you've made – or perhaps pictures you've painted.

(Business with the audience.)

Did you go and get all the right ingredients first, or just use what you'd got lying around?

(Encourage people to elaborate on their improvisations.)

Well, I'm going to tell you about the most wonderful creative adventure ever. In fact, we're going to see what no human eye has witnessed before: the creation of the world.

Imagine: it's dark. I mean, *really* dark.

And everything's just a mess – the whole universe is no more than a great big pile of rubbish, floating in an endless ocean of water. That's all there is.

> It's quiet too. Dead quiet.
>
> Except for a wind rustling on the surface of the water. Know what that is? God's own breath, that's what.
>
> Then he speaks.
>
> 'Let there be light!'
>
> Wow! Where did that come from? Brilliant light, everywhere – shining on that vast water (it's a flood light!) and showing up all the rubbish that's floating around.

God likes it. Good stuff, light. But it shows up a mess something awful.

Stories for telling

Got to do some sorting out – make space to work.

'To start with,' God says, 'we can separate the light from the dark. "Day" and "night", I'll call them.'

So there's morning, and there's evening, and what does that add up to?

One day gone.

> Then God speaks again.
>
> 'Let's get a bit of order, round here. Let's have a big dome – I'll keep some water above it and some below, and I'll call the dome "sky". Hey, it's looking better already.'
>
> But it's amazing how time flies when you're enjoying yourself.
>
> Another evening, another morning – another day gone.

God gets stuck in again. 'Let's get all that water under the sky into one place – should be some dry land in there somewhere. There it is. Right, so the water's "sea", and the dry land's "earth". Now is that great, or is that great!'

Well, God's got some space to work with, hasn't he: there'll be no holding him now! So he talks to the earth. No kidding! And it works, too.

'OK, don't just sit there – do I have to do everything myself? Give me some plants – with seeds in them! Give me some fruit trees – and don't forget the seeds in the fruit – every kind imaginable, OK?'

And the earth does it.

And God likes it.

Another evening, another morning. That's the third day.

> So, let's see – what've we got? We've got a dome for the sky . . . earth, sea . . . we've got plants and trees springing up all over the place and seeding themselves like it's a new idea – suppose it is, actually.

Let's get creative

> Makes you wonder what God's got up his sleeve next, doesn't it? (Does God have sleeves, I wonder? Well, I don't suppose it's important.)

So, God speaks again. 'Hey, that dome's a bit samey, isn't it? Can't tell day from night! Let's have some lights in it – nice bright one for the day, cool little night-light – good way of measuring this "time" stuff that I've just invented.'

So now we've got sun, moon, stars . . . that'll keep the day and the night apart. And God likes it. Another evening, another morning. Would you believe it – four days already?

> Then God speaks to the sea. Well, it worked with the earth, so why not?
>
> 'Let's have some life out of you. Come on, you know you can do it – well, with my help you can, anyway. I want living creatures everywhere – and how about some birds to fly across the sky?'
>
> Suddenly, we've got everything from hawks to halibuts, swooping and swimming for all they're worth. And monsters? I tell you, Hollywood's best special effects can't come close to this. Then God really gets carried away.
>
> 'Consider yourselves blessed!' he says. 'So, go on – spread out – reproduce!'
>
> And of course, they do. So there's not much time for anything else.
>
> Another evening, another morning – five days, I make it.

Time for God to talk to the earth again – we're getting used to this now, aren't we! 'What about you? What can you produce? Go on – wild animals, cattle, creepy crawlies – I want the lot.'

Well, that's it – suddenly we've got things running, crawling, jumping, flying, swimming and slithering all over the

Stories for telling

place. Mind your foot on that spider! And God likes it. And he decides he's on a roll and doesn't want to stop.

> 'Let's make human beings!' he says. 'Make them like us,' he says. 'Give them responsibility!' he says. And he does. Human beings – able to love, and think, and relate, able to have real meaning in their lives – like God, in fact. Men and women. 'Bless you!' he says. 'Now, go and have children, and care for this earth of mine. OK? Look, I've given you all you need: plants and trees, plenty to eat and drink – but don't forget the animals need their share, too.'

Then God takes a long look at everything: earth, sky, land, sea – plants, fruit, flowers – creatures running about everywhere – it's the biggest wildlife park in history. And he loves it. So, another evening, another morning.

Six days gone.

> All done and dusted. Well, not quite, actually. One more thing to create.
>
> Rest.
>
> Relaxation.
>
> Fun.
>
> Whatever – just as long as it's not work, because there's been quite enough of that on the six days.
>
> And God blesses that as well.

Crib sheet

What have they made/painted?
Right ingredients or improvised?
Now for the greatest creative adventure ever – first time witnessed by mortals.

Dark – mess – rubbish floating in endless water.
Quiet – except for God's breath on water.

God: 'Let there be light!' – Wow!
God likes it – but what a mess!

Need to make space (sort and separate):
- Light (day) from dark (night) – one day gone.
- Dome to separate waters (sky) – two days.
- Sea from land. God thinks it's great!

God talks to the earth: 'Produce vegetation/seeds' – three days.

God calls for lights in the sky – sun, moon, stars – four days.

God calls forth sea creatures and birds – five days.

God talks to earth again: 'Animals!'

God makes human beings – his likeness – puts them in charge.
Biggest wildlife park ever – it's all wonderful! Six days.

Then God creates rest – one day in seven – and blesses it.

We'll do it our way

Based on Genesis 3

Well, here we are. God's made a beautiful world, and he's put two people in it. Remember their names? Oddem and Even? Oh, no – Adam and Eve!

So, there they are, the only people on earth, and a beautiful garden to look after. You've never seen an orchard like it! All the fruit you can think of, and they can eat until they burst.

Well, not quite – God's put one tree off limits: the Tree of Knowing Good and Evil. 'Eat it and your dead!' he's told them.

Now, they're not actually alone. Oh, they're the only humans, all right, but the place is teeming with other creatures that God's made. Any ideas?

(Business with audience)

OK, OK, let's not get carried away. Anyway, there's one that's more cunning, more devious, more devilish crafty than all the rest of them put together. Anyone know what it is?

Snake in the grass! There it is, with its tiny beady eyes, and a big, fat sense of its own importance, just waiting to throw the nearest it's got to a big, heavy spanner right into the works. And it gets its chance when it sees Eve walking in the garden and looking a tad bored.

'Hi, Babe,' it says, 'What's this I hear about God saying you can't eat any of the fruit?' OK, you know and I know that isn't what God said, and so does the snake, but why let truth get in the way of a good opportunity?

> Eve tries to put him right. 'Oh, we can eat whatever we like,' she says. 'Just not from that tree in the middle – I mean, if we so much as take one bite we'll come over all mortal, and then we'll die. God says so.'

So, the snake puts on his reasonable voice. 'You don't want to believe everything you hear!' he tells her. 'God just can't hack the competition, that's all – you eat from that tree, you'll know all you need to know to be just like God yourselves. Of course he doesn't want you to do that – it's a power thing.'

The snake's little beady eyes are pictures of innocence – Eve can't believe he'd lie to her. And she's sure she can see a smile hovering around that flickering, forked tongue. 'Go on,' he whispers seductively. 'You know you want to. If it *feels* right, it must *be* right. Go with the flow.'

> So she does – boy, does that taste good! But before she's got a chance to wipe the juice off her chin, her husband Adam's there beside her. 'What've you done?' he's saying. 'Oh, my life – you haven't eaten from that tree? You were told not to! You know you'll die.'

Eve gets really defensive at that. 'You telling me I look dead?' she shouts at him. 'Well, thanks a bunch, Adam – the shine soon went off this marriage, didn't it!' Then her voice softens. 'It's really good, Adam – why don't you have some too?'

So there's Adam chewing away on the forbidden fruit, when suddenly he starts staring at Eve as if he's never seen her before. Then he starts spluttering: 'Hey! You're . . . you're . . . you've got no . . . you haven't . . .'

Eve gets really impatient at this. 'Oh, Adam, pull yourself together – and put some clothes on, you look ridiculous!'

Now, for some reason, they never worried about being –

Stories for telling

well, I'm sorry, but I've got to use the word – naked, before. It just didn't seem to matter. So why's it suddenly important now?

Next thing they know, they're scuttling around gathering leaves from the fig trees and joining them together to try and cover the essentials. Funny, isn't it? Five minutes earlier, they'd got nothing to hide from each other, and now they're starting to keep secrets.

But hush! What's that noise? Can't be God, can it? It is – walking in the garden, taking the evening air. And suddenly that's bad too. So they're hiding in the undergrowth trying to look like two people who aren't there, when God calls out, 'Where are you?' Adam knows the game's up.

'OK, God, you got me!' he says. 'Look, I'm sorry, OK, but I heard you coming and panicked – I mean, I'm starkers – do you blame me for hiding?'

'Oh,' says God, 'So you're starkers, are you? And why's that a problem all of a sudden? You weren't bothered about it before. Have you been eating what you shouldn't have been eating?'

Well, you've never seen anything like it: all blaming each other like politicians after an election defeat. 'Not my responsibility,' Adam says. 'It was all her – the woman – she tempted me – well, a guy can only take so much.'

The woman's not standing for that. 'Don't go blaming me,' she says. 'I was tempted too, you know – the snake did it. It's all his fault – blame him.'

By now, God's seriously not impressed. 'Temptation's one thing,' he says. 'Giving in to it's another. I suppose you both just had to do that, didn't you? Well, if you're all going to go around blaming one another every time you get things wrong, then you've really blown it. You've no idea what you've started, have you?'

So, that's that. They've got to leave the garden, of course – before they ruin that as well. And there they are, blaming each other, fighting over who did what to whom – and thousands of years later, they'll still be at it – them and all their children. Still doing things their way – still blaming everyone else when it goes wrong – still refusing to take responsibility.

People!

Don't you just love 'em!

Stories for telling

Crib sheet

Well, here we are – beautiful world, Oddem and Even (sorry – Adam and Eve), garden, orchard, fruit . . .

One tree's off limits – 'Eat it and die!'

> Snake – craftiest of all animals – homes in on Eve: 'Can't you eat the fruit?'
>
> Conversation: 'We'll die.' 'You won't – God can't hack the competition.' Persuasive.

Eve tastes it – gorgeous. Offers it to Adam.

Suddenly, Adam notices that Eve's naked! She makes similar observation about Adam.

> Fig-leaf foxtrot interrupted by God – 'Who told you you were naked?'
>
> All blame one another – complete breakdown in relationships.

So they're thrown out of the garden. Thousands of years later, their children will still be blaming each other – no one takes responsibility!

Remember the rainbow

Based on Genesis 6-9

Let me take you back to the old, old days when the world was young. Young, but not very nice.

Well, here we are. Actually, the *world* is wonderful – it's the *people* that are the problem: selfish, cruel, and a complete disgrace to their creator.

God decides it can't go on. 'I'm sorry I made this lot!' he says. 'Let's get rid of them and start again.' So that's it – every living creature's gong to be obliterated.

Well, actually, not quite. There is one good family – Noah's. He's got a wife and three sons – Shem, Ham and Japheth. And they're OK. Which is why God decides to save them, to make a fresh start.

And that's how Noah comes to be building a boat – a big one – big enough for himself, his family and a pair of every kind of animal, bird and creepy thing you can imagine.

So, here we all are, snug as a bug in a rug – and we've got a selection of those too – when God makes it rain. Then after that he makes it rain. And after it's rained he makes it rain.

Wet? Even the mountains are drowned! And there's Noah, with – oh, what were his sons' names, again?*

Thank you! Well, there they are, in a floating safari park.

---

* Let the audience help you out.

17

Stories for telling

The novelty soon wears off, as you might imagine, and Noah sends one of the ravens out looking for land. No luck. It just ends up flying round and round trying to find a perch. Next, he sends a dove out – but it comes back because there's no land.

Another week goes by – off goes the dove again. This time, it comes back with an olive twig in its beak. So what do you think that means?*

So, they wait again – Noah, and his wife, and his sons, Shed, Bacon and Jaffa† – and a week later off goes the dove again. This time it doesn't come back.

Time to open the hatches. Wow – fresh air! I bet that's a relief to whoever's been mucking out the elephants. Hey, folks, there's dry land out there! Then they hear God speaking.

'Well, don't just stand there sniffing – get out: you and all the animals. You've got to spread out all over the world and start things off again.'

And they do! In no time the world's full of life. Some of the creatures take a while to find their land-legs again – especially the centipedes – but soon you can't move without something running, hopping, crawling or flapping out of the way.

And let's not forget the humans: Noah, and his wife, and those other three, Thingy, Wossname and Hoozit?‡ Yes, they're the ones – just testing. God's got a special word to say to them.

'Never again!' he says. 'Never again will I cause a flood like this one, to destroy all the world. Look – up in the sky – what do you see?'

---

* The tree-tops are showing above the water!
† Wrong again! Let them remind you.
‡ Give the listeners time to correct you.

Noah looks and he saw a – oh, you know – a bow thing.*
Yes, that's it. Anyway, there's all this beautiful coloured light. 'That's a reminder of my promise,' God says. 'A sign of the love I have for you. When things get rough, remember the rainbow.'

And we do.

---

* Wait for the prompt!

Stories for telling

Crib sheet

> Imagine living in a zoo: what would it be like?
> (*Let them answer.*)

Back to the old days when the world was young – but not nice (world OK – people not nice!).

God decides to wipe it all out – except Noah's family – good people. Son's names: Shem, Ham and Japheth.

Noah builds a boat – for his family and other animals.

> Rain! There they all are – forgotten sons' names!
> Noah sends out raven – finds no land. Dove, likewise.
> Week later – dove – returns with olive branch.

They wait another week: Noah, wife and Shed, Bacon and Jaffa.

Dove out again – doesn't return. Time to open hatches. Fresh air!

God speaks: Go out and fill the world with life. They do – and how!

> Don't forget the humans: Noah, wife, Thingy, Wossname and Hoozit. Special promise for them:
> God will never again destroy whole world with flood.

Rainbow.

When things get rough, remember the rainbow.

Towering ambition

Based on Genesis 11:1-9

What do you reckon is the tallest building in the world?
- The Empire State Building in New York? Doesn't come close!
- What about the International Finance centre in Hong Kong? Short by 257 metres!

Unless this has changed recently, it's the Centre of India Tower, in Katangi, India – and it's 677 metres tall! That's 2222 feet, and 224 storeys!*

Now don't laugh, but some of us remember the time when we thought Big Ben was a tall building.

Me, I blame it on Lego – once you go encouraging children to put one thing on top of another – and they find out that it doesn't actually need to fall over – you just don't know where it'll end.

According to the Bible, however, people got the tall buildings bug thousands of years ago.

It all begins – as most silliness does – with someone whose ego is bigger than their brain. I mean, it's all going quite well – people speaking the same language, understanding one another (up to a point, anyway) and generally rubbing along together (well, after a fashion) – and then some overgrown kid with his building blocks gets carried away.

---

* That's according to the table 'World's Tallest Buildings' in Encarta 2002 – you might like to check for updates!

Stories for telling

'Let's build a tower!' he says. 'Let's make a stairway to heaven – we can go and take a peek at the angels, see the sights, get to know the stars – it'll be well good, that will. Be a great bit of security, too – nothing like a nice, tall tower to make you feel good, is there!'

Now, the trouble with people like that is *other* people – other people who listen to them. So, before you can say, 'International Building Regulations section five, subsection three, paragraph 32' they've got all the latest lifting gear (ramps, levers and wooden rollers) and are piling stones on top of one another like nothing else matters.

Well, God decides it's time he took a closer look, so he pops down one night when it's all quiet, to do a site inspection. And it's not a pretty site. 'Not happy with this,' he murmurs. 'Not happy at all – the quality's far too good for a job of this kind. I mean, where's it going to end? Give them a couple of days – well, a few thousand years in their time – and the world'll be full of great tall towers, with long-range lenses poking over the top, all aimed at my Throne Room. Paparazzi in Paradise – doesn't bear thinking about – sounds like the title for a really cringe-making movie (and they'll find out about those soon enough without any encouragement). Well, there's only one thing for it. Better get back to the office and make a few calls.'

By the next morning, everything's sorted out, and the place is looking every inch the dynamic, modern building project that humans are so proud of. In other words, chaos – absolute, unmitigated, unapologetic, chaos. Everyone's shouting at everyone else and no one's understanding what's being said to them. And if that doesn't sound familiar to you, then you haven't worked in some of the places I have. In this case, though, it's really serious. They're speaking completely different languages; what one person says sounds like total gibberish to another. And, yes, I know you don't need to speak a different language for that to happen – but you have to admit it helps.

Towering ambition

Anyway – that's the end of the great tower project. The job's left half-finished – a situation not unfamiliar to a fair number of us, I expect – just sitting there as a mute, morose symbol of things to come. And the people? Well, you can't go on living together when you don't all speak the same language, can you? At least, that's what *they* think. Me, I'm not so sure. Everywhere I go, there are houses filled with men, women, children, teenagers, who all seem to be speaking entirely different languages and somehow manage to get along together pretty well. But I digress.

Unfortunately, our friends at the tower don't have the prophetic vision to foresee that possibility, so they all decide to pack it in and go live somewhere else. So, they disappear off to the ends of the earth, carrying their laundry, languages and limitations with them.

Trouble is, they take something else too – their penchant for vertically elongated architecture. I know I shouldn't say this, but I think God's scheme backfired more than somewhat – I mean, go to almost any part of the world you like and you'll find some overgrown adolescent with a hard hat where his school cap should be, playing with his life-size Lego and trying to build a taller tower than the last one.

Isn't 677 metres enough for anybody?

Stories for telling

Crib sheet

What do you reckon is the tallest building in the world?
- The Empire State Building in New York? Doesn't come close!
- What about the International Finance centre in Hong Kong? Short by 257 metres!

> Unless this has changed recently, it's the Centre of India Tower, in Katangi, India – and it's 677 metres tall! That's 2,222 feet, and 224 storeys!

Don't laugh – Big Ben.

All down to Lego.

> Tall buildings bug caught thousands of years ago.
>
> Things OK – one language – people get along. Until ...
>
> 'Let's build a tower – angels – stars – prestige and security.' Soon, everything's under way.

God does site inspection – not a pretty site. Paparazzi in Paradise. Better do something.

Next morning – absolute chaos. Everyone shouting, no one understanding – sound familiar? Completely different languages – sounds like utter gibberish.

Project ends – all split up and go to other places – can't live together if you can't communicate!

> Trouble is – they take their ambitions with them. Dare I say that God's plan seems to have backfired? Now there are overgrown children building tall buildings all over the world!

Isn't 677 metres enough for anybody?

In your dreams, Jacob!

Based on Genesis 28:11-22

This is a story about a dream that comes true. And it happens to someone who definitely doesn't deserve it: Jacob.

He's not a nice man – he's just taken advantage of his old and dying father, Isaac, to con his own brother out of his inheritance. Esau – that's his brother – is hopping mad, and I for one don't blame him, and Jacob's running away.

Not stopping to face the music like a man. Running away. That's the kind of guy he is.

So, there's Jacob, on his way from Beer-sheba to Haran (don't ask me where those places are – let's just say they're a long way east of Dover). Anyway, it's late, and he's tired, so he decides to camp for the night. And what a night it's going to be!

First of all, he finds a stone for a pillow – yes, well, sometimes campers can't be choosers – and settles down to sleep.

Gradually, his eyelids get heavy . . . and heavier . . . and heavier . . . And they start to close . . . and gently, he drifts off to sleep.

Tan-tara-tara!

Who the heck's playing the trumpet at this time of night! And who put that ladder there?

No kidding – there's this great big ladder, stretching up from the earth right to heaven, and angels going up and down on it.

Stories for telling

And that's not all. Just who do you think is standing beside Jacob, looking as if this was all perfectly usual?

God.

No, really – God. Big G himself, come to pay Jacob a visit. Well, they say God never sleeps, so perhaps this is as good a time as any.

'Hi, Jacob – I'm God, see? You remember me, don't you? The God of your granddaddy Abraham, and Isaac? Well, I'm telling you what I told them. See this land – this land where you're trying to get some sleep? Well, it's yours – I'm giving it to you and to your children. Did I say children? Man, I really mean children like no one's ever had before. Thousands of them – like the dust on the ground! I mean, you're going to be just all over the place. The whole world's going to be blessed – and, man, do I mean blessed – because of you!'

Now, Jacob's still trying to get his head round the game of seraphs and ladders that's going on in front of his eyes – but God just goes right on talking.

'Now, know this, Jakey, baby: you don't get away from me that easily. Wherever you go, I'll be there, taking care of you. You go away from this land, I'll bring you back to it. And whether you deserve it or not, I'm not giving up on you until I've kept my promise. That's the kind of God I am.'

Then Jacob wakes up. Well, you would, wouldn't you?

'Well, I'll go to the foot of our stairs!' he says. 'God's right here in this place, and I didn't know anything about it.'

Now, that's a serious proposition, you know? A bit more than Jacob's planned for. This is where the skin turns clammy, and the breathing gets shallower, and the old knees get the shakes. 'This place is awesome!' he says. 'I mean, seriously – this is the house of God, no less. This is the gate of heaven itself.'

In your dreams, Jacob!

So what does he do? He gets up, picks up the stone he's used for a pillow and sets it up as a pillar – then he pours oil on it to show that it's holy. He renames the place Bethel – never mind that it already has a name, Luz – and he makes a promise.

'OK, OK, so God's calling the tune. Well, that's fine by me – you keep your side of it and I'll keep mine. Let me make peace with my family, and I'll be completely faithful to you from then on. I've set up this pillar, see – just for you, God – your place. Help me do well in life, and I'll give ten per cent to you.'

So, what do you think? Will Jacob keep his promise and go straight?

Well, he's always going to be a bit of a rogue – he'll get things wrong often enough. But you see the really wonderful thing in this story is this:

It's not about how good Jacob is. It's about how good *God* is. Even when we don't deserve it.

Stories for telling

Crib sheet

A dream comes true – for undeserving Jacob!

Not a nice man – conned his dying father and his older brother – now he's running away.

That's our Jacob!

Stops for the night – finds a stone to use for a pillow. Goes to sleep.

'Tarantara!'

Ladder – stretching from heaven to earth – angels.

God speaks – reaffirms his promise to Abraham – land – children – a blessing to the whole world.

And there's more: God will always be with him, no matter what – 'That's the kind of God I am.'

Then Jacob wakes up. All a bit overwhelming. 'This place is awesome – house of God – gate of heaven!'

Sets up and anoints a pillar – calls the place Bethel – promises to tithe.

Will he keep his word?

Really wonderful thing – it's all about God's goodness, not Jacob's.

Moses in the rushes

Based on Exodus 2:1-10

Right: we've got the Israelites and the Egyptians – OK?

The Israelites are immigrants in Egypt and they're doing a bit too well for their own good – in some places there seem to be more Israelites than Egyptians. So, the natives are getting twitchy.
- What if they do better than us?
- What if they take over – with all their strange ways and odd customs?
- And have you had a whiff of their cooking?

Then the king – Pharaoh, they call him – well, he decides to do something about it. Make them into slaves, he thinks – give them all the lousy jobs to do for no pay – that'll keep them in their place.

Know what? Doesn't work.

Every year there are more of them – and the ill treatment just makes them angrier.
- What if they raise an army – take over the country completely?
- What if they then treat 'us' the way we treat 'them' now?

Pharaoh has another brilliant idea. It's the men that are the dangerous ones, not the women – he doesn't know much, does he! – so let's kill all the boy babies at birth, and then they'll never be able to grow up into fighters.

Clever stuff! Well, that's what *he* thinks, anyway.

Stories for telling

Boy, has he got a rude awakening coming!

> So, there's this Israelite family, and they've got a baby boy – just born, still under warranty.
>
> What are they going to do – can't let Pharaoh's mob get their paws on him, can they?
>
> Well, the first three months are OK – they keep the baby hidden. But you know as well as I do that as babies get older, they get disproportionately louder – for about the first 19 years or so.
>
> So, by the time he's three months old, the child can't be kept secret any more.
>
> Now, here's where they get really clever – well, cleverer than Pharaoh, anyway, but that's not difficult, now I come to think about it. They make a floating cradle out of reeds, waterproof it with tar, and hide the baby among the rushes at the side of the River Nile.
>
> And just to be on the safe side, the baby's big sister, Miriam, hides nearby to keep watch.

Uh-oh – here's trouble. Pharaoh's daughter, complete with servants, bubble bath and fluffy bathrobe, coming to take a dip in the river. And, of course, she sees the cradle and finds the baby.

Well, luckily she's not like her dad and she goes dewy-eyed over the child. 'Must be a slave-child,' she says. 'Oo's a priddy, priddy liddle baby, den?'

The baby, understandably, refuses to dignify that with a response, but the princess decides she'll keep him and bring him up to know better.

> Now, don't forget, Miriam's watching all this from a safe distance. What's she going to do? She'd put the baby there for safety, and now he's going to finish up sleeping with the enemy.

Moses in the rushes

> Quick as a flash, she's there. 'Um, 'scuse me, Your Highness – nice baby – reckon you'll be needing a nurse? I know just the person – how about it?'
>
> Well, the princess agrees and Miriam goes haring back home to get her mother. The Princess then gives the baby back to his own mother and tells her to look after him.
>
> Now, that *is* clever.

Then when the baby's old enough not to be a problem, the princess decides she'll take over. And just to make sure everyone understands that he's now *her* baby, she gives him a name.

'I drew him out of the water,' she says. So I'll call him "Drawn out".'

Now, did you ever hear a name like that? I mean, can you imagine some poor child growing up with a name like 'Drawn out'? Well, fortunately, the Egyptian word for that was 'Moses', which sounds a whole lot better to me.

> Now, what none of them realised was that God had a cunning plan. This delightful little boy, growing up in the Pharaoh's palace, was going to end up leading a revolution.

But that's another story.

Stories for telling

Crib sheet

Israelites and the Egyptians.

Egyptians afraid of immigrants doing too well – enslave them.

Doesn't work – they just get angrier – and more dangerous.

Pharaoh's grand plan: kill all the boy babies. No boys now means no warriors later.

Israelite family have a baby boy and hide him for three months – then make a basket and hide him in reeds by the river bank. Sister, Miriam, keeps watch.

Pharaoh's daughter finds him – decides to keep him.

Miriam gets her mother employed as wet-nurse!

As the boy grows up, the princess names him 'Drawn out' (of the water).

Luckily, the Egyptian word is 'Moses' – that's better.

Future liberator of the Israelites growing up in Pharaoh's palace!

But that's another story.

A burning desire for freedom
Based on Exodus 3:1-15

I tell you, you've never seen anything like it in your life. I don't care if you've seen pyramids, pyrotechnics or penguins in pantaloons – you've never seen anything quite like this.

It all begins with Moses. He's out in the desert, minding sheep for his father-in-law, Jethro. Now, that's a bit of a come-down for someone who's grown up as the adopted grandson of the king of Egypt – but all that came to an end when Moses realised he was really an Israelite, sided with the slaves and killed an Egyptian slave-driver. Well, you don't do that and then just wander back home and say, 'Hi, Mum – what's for tea?' now do you?

> So, there he is – minding the sheep, his own business and how he crosses the road – when he sees this amazing sight. A bush nearby is on fire – blazing away like mad. But the strange thing is it's not burning up. Well, naturally, Moses is a bit curious. What sort of bush is this? He goes a little closer to get a better look, and that's when it happens. It speaks to him. No kidding! Well, actually, it's God who speaks from it. Oh, so that's what kind of bush it is – a God bush – which is at least one up on a president bush.

God pulls him up short. 'Hey, hey, hey, hold on a minute there – just where do you think you're going in that footwear?' Moses is just wondering what's wrong with his footwear (after all, a shoe's a shoe, isn't it – no one's heard of Reebok, yet) when God says, 'Get them off – and quickly – this is holy ground you're on. I'm God, see – and not just any dime-a-dozen idol, either. I'm the God of your ancestors – Abraham, Isaac, Jacob – remember now?'

Stories for telling

By now, Moses has forgotten all about the bush and has got his face well and truly buried in his cloak – which, when God's around, is to a religious person as sand is to an ostrich. You just don't go looking at God as if he's a creature in a zoo – OK?

'Look,' God tells him, ' – well, listen, anyway – I've been listening to my people in Egypt, and I don't like what I'm hearing. No, sir, I don't. I know they're being bullied and exploited – I know they're miserable – and I've come here to get them out of it. So, that's where you come in. You're going to go to Pharaoh and tell him to let them go.'

By now Moses is wishing he'd never shown an interest. 'Go to whom? And tell him what? You do realise that the only difference between Pharaoh and a nest of angry spitting cobras is that you can reason with angry spitting cobras? No, you've got the wrong guy – you want someone suitable. I'm not suitable – I've been called a lot of things in my life, but suitable isn't one of them.'

God's had enough. 'Moses, why do you think I gave you only one mouth but two ears? You've used the former, so now shut it and let the latter work a double shift. I'm not sending you alone – I'm going to be with you all the way. You're going to do it, old lad – trust me – before you know it, you'll all be up here on this mountain worshipping me.'

Well, it sounds as if God's had the last word. But, as they say, it's not over until the fat lady sings – and right now there isn't a generously proportioned woman within earshot. So Moses decides to give it another go. 'Look,' he says, 'you understand the difficulty, don't you? I mean, *I* know who you are, but back in Egypt they've all forgotten you. Careless of them, of course, but there it is. So they're going to ask me who's sent me, and I don't know what to tell them. I mean, have you got a name, or a cyber-space reference code or something?'

Now, God's not falling for that. Even through his cloak, Moses can see the bush flaring up angrily. 'Name? Name?

A burning desire for freedom

You think you can define me – explain me – confine me in some mortal category and think you understand me? Well, listen, and listen good – and don't even *think* of correcting my grammar – I'll be what and who *I* decide to be. You got that? You just go to the Israelites and tell them that The One Who Is has sent you to them. They don't need to know any more than that – but that won't stop them asking awkward questions; so just say that the God of your ancestors, Abraham, Isaac and Jacob, has sent you. That's the nearest to a name that I'm ever going to give myself – and I mean, ever. You go and tell them that. Then let's set them free.'

Well, it might be wishful thinking, but by now Moses is sure he can hear the distant sound of singing: the song of the fat lady. It's over – time to give in gracefully and go.

Stories for telling

Crib sheet

You've never seen anything like it!

Begins with Moses – shepherding in the desert – rather a comedown for the king of Egypt's adopted grandson, but he's an Israelite at heart.

Also wanted for murder.

Bush – on fire, but not burning up. Moses goes closer.

God: 'Take your shoes off – holy ground – God of ancestors.'

Moses hides face. God continues: heard prayers – will save his people.

Moses: 'You want someone suitable – not me!'

God: 'I'll be with you.'

It's not over till the fat lady sings. Moses: 'People have forgotten you – what name shall I say?'

God: 'No names, no labels, no restrictive definitions – I'll be who I decide to be. God of your ancestors. Tell them that – set them free.'

Now, the fat lady *is* singing. Time to give in gracefully and do it!

Just walk this way

Based on Exodus 14:5-31

We're going back to a long time ago – not just a few hours, not just a few years, not even just a few hundred years. It's thousands of years ago, and the people of Israel have just run away from the wicked king of Egypt. Not a nice man, the king of Egypt – he made all the foreign people in his country work as slaves. So, they've run away. And Moses is their leader.

Well, I say Moses – Moses is their human leader, but it's God who's really showing the way. He's put a big cloud in front for them to follow, and at night it turns into fire so they can see it and know which way to go.

> Well, so far, so good. They've trekked through the desert until they've come to the shores of the Red Sea, and now they're having a rest. But while they're resting, what do you think's happening back in Egypt? Do you think the people are happy that their slaves have run away?

They've got to do their own cooking. They've got to wash their own clothes, do their own shopping (anything else?).

So, they start moaning. And they go to the king. And what do you think they say?

'Get them back!' they tell him. 'We want our slaves back here to work for us,' they tell him. 'You've got to send out the army,' they tell him.

So, he does. Anything for a quiet life.

Stories for telling

> So there are the runaway slaves, camped by the seaside cooling their feet, and they notice something . . .
> - a cloud of dust on the horizon,
> - rumbling in the ground, like chariot wheels,
> - horses' hooves drumming.
>
> What's happening?
>
> The Egyptians are coming to get them! And they've got nowhere to run away to, except into the sea!

Now, that's seriously frightening. But they don't panic. Oh, no – panic would be quite mild.

They skip that stage and go straight into an absolute flat spin: running around yelling and screaming at one another.

Then they stop yelling and screaming at one another. That's not going to do any good, is it?

> So they start yelling and screaming at Moses instead.
>
> Moses doesn't panic, though. He talks to God about it, and God tells him what to do.
>
> Moses goes down to the seashore, and God moves the cloud from in front of the camp to behind it – between them and the Egyptians.

Then Moses raises his hand and stretches out his arm towards the water. As soon as he does that, God sends a really strong wind, and it blows down into the sea.

Does anybody know what that does?

It begins to drive the water apart. Very gradually, though. All through the night, Moses is standing there like a signpost pointing at the sea, and little by little, hour by hour, the channel made by the wind is getting deeper – until by morning you can see the sea bed.

> Then Moses calls the people. 'Get your gear, and get over here!' he shouts at them.

Just walk this way

> Well, you might be able to imagine how they feel. What've they got? A path to walk along to get to the other side of the sea. Sound OK? Well, what about the water – two great big walls of it, one each side, foaming and swirling in the wind – and what a wind it must be!
>
> So, let's get this straight: Moses wants them to walk the whole way to the other side, with a howling gale blowing, and with tons of water piled up on each side and only the wind to keep it that way!
>
> Oh, sure. Think again, Moses!

But, then, what else can they do?

Because as well as the wind, they can hear something else: d-dum, d-dum, d-dum – the sound of horses' hooves – thousands of them – echoing through the ground. The Egyptian army. And it's coming for them!

The people start to drag their animals and their belongings down to the shore, and one by one they pluck up the courage and step into that horrible alleyway between the water.

- The wind's blowing.*
- The sea's roaring and raging.
- The people are screaming in fear.
- And all the time the Egyptian horses and chariots are thundering toward them.

For hours they walk between those walls of water, cursing the wind because it keeps blowing them over, and yet praying it doesn't stop. Because if it does, what's going to happen to all that water?

> Then someone shouts, 'Land! I can see land! We're almost there!' And they start to move more quickly. They think

---

* Children may like to make the sounds.

Stories for telling

> they might not make it – the water sounds angry, as if it doesn't want them to escape. Maybe it doesn't like being pinned back like that by the wind.

Eventually all the people are across.

Well, the wicked king of Egypt thinks that anything they can do he can do better – so he thinks he's going to go through there after them.

What do you think? No chance.

An ant would have more chance of moving a mountain than he's got of doing that. A fish would fly to the moon before the Egyptians could get through that water.

Why? Well, remember who it was that opened up that path in the first place?

God. Exactly. And what God can open, God can close.

So, what does God do? He turns off the wind. Simple as that.

And without the wind, what's going to happen to that pathway?

Exactly. You never heard a noise like it when all that water came crashing back together again. I bet you can't *make* a sound like it, either!

So, that's how God got the Israelites finally beyond the reach of the wicked king and his lazy people. *They* are going to have to do their own washing up for a very long time.

Just walk this way

Crib sheet

Back a long time – not hours or years or centuries – thousands of years.

Israelites escaping from slavery in Egypt led by Moses – well, God, actually – pillar of cloud.

Arrive at shore of Red Sea.

> Meanwhile, Egyptians not happy – send army after them.
>
> Israelites notice: dust, wheels rumbling, hooves drumming.
>
> Trapped! They don't panic – they miss out that stage! Yelling and screaming at each other – then at Moses.

Moses reaches out over the sea – pillar of cloud moves behind them.

Wind – gradually deepens the channel until seabed appears.

Moses: 'Come on!' He's got to be joking! But there's no choice.

- wind blowing
- sea roaring
- people screaming
- chariots and hooves thundering

> Then the journey – more sound effects!
>
> They get across, Egyptians think they can follow.
>
> God turns off the wind.
>
> Egyptians will have to do their own washing up from now on.

God feeds his people

Based on Exodus 16:2-25

Picture the scene: God's set the Israelite slaves free, led them out into the desert on their way to a land of their own, and everybody's moaning about Moses and his brother, Aaron. On and on they go at Moses. 'Why didn't this wonderful God of yours just kill us off in Egypt?' they're yelling at him. 'We could have died happy there, with the nightlife, the food, the drink – why'd you have to bring us out into this lousy place to die of hunger?'

Well, talk about romanticising the past – all this stuff about nightlife, and food! They were slaves when they were in Egypt, and the closest they'd ever have got to going clubbing would be mopping the floor after the joint had closed – probably with their tongues. Now they're free people on their journey to the promised land. Well, that's the theory, but it looks to me like they've got an awful lot of growing up to do before it becomes a reality.

Anyway, God decides it's time to get involved. Personally. 'OK, Moses,' he says. 'They want bread – I'll make it *rain* bread! They'll be picking it up off the ground, every day. And even then – well, let's just see whether they take any notice of me. Oh, and you know what I told you about not working on day seven? Well, on every sixth day I'll rain you two days' supply so that you don't have to.'

So Moses and Aaron go and make the announcement. 'Now, listen, you lot, and listen well. Come this evening, God's going to show you who's really in charge of this operation. Remember God, the one who set you free from

God feeds his people

Egypt and you've done nothing but moan about? Well, by tomorrow morning you'll be singing his praises – because he's heard all your whingeing and your complaining about him. Oh, yes, it's him you've been moaning about, not us, because he's the big cheese around here – well, around everywhere, really. I mean, who do you think we are to take responsibility for everything – your nursemaids, or something? You just wait and see – when God gives you meat to eat in the evening, and fills you up with bread from heaven for breakfast, because he's taken notice of your complaints – then you'll realise that Aaron and I are nothing. It's God you've been shouting at, not us!'

> A little bit later Moses says to Aaron, 'Get the people together. Tell them to come and face the God they've been moaning about – because he's heard them.' Well, even as Aaron starts making his speech, the people look out into the desert, and what do you think they see? Only the glory of God himself, shining in a great, bright cloud, that's all! Then, if that wasn't terrifying enough, God speaks. 'I've heard all the complaints,' he says, 'and now I'm going to do something about them. Tell them to break out the best earthenware, because it's dinner time. You're going to have meat tonight – yes, folks, fresh poultry's on the menu. Meat tonight, and bread for breakfast tomorrow. I'll show you who's God around here!'

OK, I know what you're thinking – they're out in the desert, miles from any towns and three thousand years from the first refrigerator – where's God going to get meat to feed an entire nation?

Africa – that's where. No kidding. And he doesn't have a transport problem because it flies itself in. We're talking migrating quails, here – thousands of them – so tired after a long flight that they just flop on to the ground and wait to be picked up. And, that's the meat taken care of. Then, in the morning, there's this strange, white-ish, sort of frosty stuff on the ground.

Stories for telling

So, what are the Israelites doing? Standing round, scratching their heads, wondering what it is. 'I'll tell you what it is,' Moses tells them. 'It's bread, that's what – the bread that God's given you to eat.'

Now, you'd think that'd stop them moaning for good, wouldn't you?

Well, it doesn't.

But that's another story.

God feeds his people

Crib sheet

Israelites are in the desert moaning – remembering Egypt – 'nightlife', 'food'! As if!

They were slaves in Egypt! Now they're free (in theory . . .).

> God promises it'll rain bread.
>
> Moses and Aaron tell the people – God will be glorified.

It's really God they've been complaining about – he's in charge – Moses and Aaron just aren't that important!

Aaron calls the people together – announcement: It's dinner time! Meat tonight, bread for breakfast.

Migrating quails fall into the camp – exhausted and vulnerable.

> Next morning, strange looking deposits on the ground. What is it?
>
> Moses tells them: it's the bread God promised.

That should stop their moaning – but it won't!

That's another story.

Now, take it easy, God!
Based on Exodus 32:1-24

I'm going to tell you about someone who argued with God to change his mind about something. Now, that may seem a bit of a cheek to you – telling the Almighty he needs to stop and think – but I reckon you need to be on pretty good terms with someone to do that. It takes a lot of trust and faith to talk to God in that way, and Moses is one of a few people in the Bible who seem to have had what it takes.

> It all begins with the Israelite people in the desert, during the time that God was using Moses to lead them to freedom. And as the story starts Moses is nowhere to be seen. So, where is he? Up a mountain, talking to God – that's where. Well, to be really honest, if I had the job of leading that lot I'd probably go up a mountain and never come down. If we drop in on what they're doing, you'll see what I mean.

While Moses is up the mountain, the people are having a go at his brother, Aaron. 'Where's Moses?' they're yelling at him. 'Gone where we can't find him – that's where. For all we know, he's never going to come back. So, why don't you give us a proper god – one we can see, touch and get a grip on!'

Now, Aaron is supposed to be exercising a bit of leadership, but he's something of a traditionalist where politics are concerned, and knows better than to stand up to the mob. 'OK, OK, whatever you say!' he sighs. 'Give me all your gold – you know, earrings, nose-rings, cakehole zips, that kind of thing.' So they do – and Aaron gets to work.

Now, take it easy, God!

> Now, I want you to listen to this next bit carefully – you might like to compare it with the way Aaron tells the story to Moses, later. Aaron takes all the gold the people have given him, and he makes a mould in just the right shape and size. Very careful, he is. And when the mould's just right, he melts the gold and pours it in. So, what's going to come out of a calf-shaped mould? Got it in one: a calf.

The people were well pleased. 'Look,' they said, 'here's the god that brought us out of slavery in Egypt and set us free.' Interesting, that. I mean, apart from the fact that this is something they've made themselves, they seem also to have forgotten that when they left Egypt it was no more than a gleam in their noses and ears.

They don't stop there, though – oh, no! Aaron gets really carried away and builds an altar to the monstrosity. Think he's gone too far now? Well, he hasn't even started! Next bright idea is to declare a public holiday so that everyone can spend the whole day worshipping the thing. The worship, of course, includes an awful lot of food, drink and good, pious debauchery – well, I suppose there has to be something in it for them, doesn't there?

> Meanwhile, Moses is up the mountain with God – the real one, that is – and neither of them is happy about things. 'You'd better get back down there, pronto,' God tells Moses. 'Those people you led out of slavery in Egypt – well, they're getting to be a real letdown and no mistake. They've only made an enormous statue of a calf and started to worship it instead of me. I mean, I've been expected to play second fiddle to some odd things, but a gold calf! Really! Well, that's it. No more Mr Nice God. You'd better get clear of me so I can let fly. I'll marmalise them – I'll vaporise them – I'll bury them so deep they'll be fossilised. By the time I've finished with that crowd of – '

At this point, Moses decides he'd better get a word in while he still can. 'Um, excuse me, God,' he says. 'Don't get me

Stories for telling

wrong, now, I mean, I know you're the Great I AM, and all that stuff, and I don't really like mentioning it, but – well, I was just thinking: you can't really be that angry with them, can you? I mean, not with the people you rescued from Egypt with your own hand? And even if you could, do you really want to give the Egyptians the satisfaction? You must be able to see the headlines: 'ISRAELITE GOD SAVES AND THEN MASSACRES HIS PEOPLE'. You know what they'll say – that you pretended to save them just so you could bring them here and enjoy destroying them! Think about it, Lord, you don't want that kind of publicity, do you? Why not do the big thing and forgive them? You know it makes sense. I mean, I don't have to remind you of what you promised Abraham, and Isaac, and Jacob, now do I? Come on, you know you've got it in you. Give them another chance – what do you say?'

> Well, believe it or not, God says, 'Yes.' So, Moses wipes away the cold sweat and goes down the mountain, carrying the stone slabs he's been using to take dictation from God – you know, the Ten Commandments – and finds the people having fun like there's a world fun shortage coming. Well, for someone who's just told God to calm down, he doesn't exactly practise what he preaches – he loses it completely, smashes the stone slabs and then makes for the calf. He goes completely OTT with that – grinds it down and makes the people mix the gold dust with their drinks. That'll show them it's not tasty enough to be God, I suppose.

The bit I like comes right at the end, though – when Moses asks Aaron to explain what happened. 'Well, it was a funny thing,' Aaron says. 'You'll laugh when I tell you. They wanted a god, so they gave me their gold. I just threw it on to the fire, the way you do, and – well, it was amazing – this calf sort of popped out of the flames.'

Now, you and I know it wasn't quite like that, don't we? Something tells me that someone is trying to avoid taking responsibility. Perhaps Aaron should take a leaf out of God's book – and listen to Moses!

Now, take it easy, God!

Crib sheet

Story about someone arguing to change God's mind – what a relationship of trust and faith!

Israelites in the desert – on way to freedom – Moses up a mountain talking to God.

> People go to Aaron: 'Moses has gone – give us a proper god – one we can hold!'
>
> Aaron – politician – submits to the mob: 'Give me your gold.'

Listen carefully – compare this bit with how Aaron tells it later. Aaron makes mould, melts gold, pours in, etc. – produces a calf.

People delighted: 'This is our god who rescued us!'

Aaron gets carried away – altar – public holiday – big festival.

> Up mountain, God tells Moses what's going on. No more Mr Nice God.
>
> Moses: 'Do you really want to give the Egyptians that kind of opportunity to mock?'

God says OK – Moses carries law slabs down mountain but doesn't practise what he's just preached to God! Smashes slabs, grinds down calf, mixes gold dust with drinking water.

Aaron: 'I just threw the gold on the fire and out came this calf'!

Talk about not taking responsibility! Be like God, Aaron – listen to Moses!

He's the greatest – honest!

Based on 1 Samuel 16:1-13

Anyone going to tell me who Muhammed Ali is?

He called himself 'The Greatest'. Oh, he was good – and not only as a boxer, either. A sharp mind and a quick wit that could strike fear into tough television interviewers.

Now, who's 'the King'? Elvis Presley? You have to admit, the man was good at what he did.

Well, let me tell you about a great king – some people still think he was the greatest.

It begins with God deciding he's had it up to here with King Saul, who was the first ever king of Israel, and it's time to replace him. Don't get me wrong – Saul's a pretty impressive sort of guy: tall, strong, good looking, fast on his feet – don't know whether he can sing, though.

The problem is, he has this really bad habit of doing things his way, not God's. So God decides he's due for early retirement – but first he needs to have a replacement lined up.

So the first person God needs to talk to is Samuel, the prophet. 'Now, see here, Sammy,' he says, 'moaning on about Saul isn't going to change anything. It's time for action – so get your anointing oil and let's move it. We're going to Bethlehem – Jesse's place – I've got the next king all lined up for you.'

Samuel isn't impressed. 'If I didn't know you were God, I'd think you'd lost it,' he says. 'If Saul gets wind of this, he'll kill me – and that'll be the kind bit.'

He's the greatest – honest!

'So play it canny,' God says. 'Take a calf with you and say you've come to offer a sacrifice to me. Oh, do I have to spell it out? Look, invite Jesse to come to the service, and then I'll show you what to do next, and which one you're to anoint. Trust me, Sam – have I ever let you down?'

So that's how Samuel finds himself going to Jesse's place with his oil in his hand, a calf at his side, and a frown on his face.

> He's hardly within sight of the city when the dignitaries are running to meet him to check that he's not going to make trouble for them. Politicians, you see – get jumpy when prophets are around. Samuel just says, 'Hey, guys, chill out! I've come to make a sacrifice – why do you think the calf's got a long face! You can come too, if you like – but go and make yourselves presentable first.'

So: Jesse's place. Samuel gets Jesse to call his sons to the service too – probably thinks he can get it all over with and then scuttle back to somewhere safer before Saul hears and hits the panic button. Well, he's in for a disappointment there. First son along: Eliab. Good looking guy, and no mistake. 'Great,' thinks Samuel. 'This is the one!'

'Not so fast, Sammy baby!' God tells him. 'Oh, he's impressive enough on the outside, but I look inside – at the heart.'

'Rather you than me,' Samuel thinks, and waits for the next candidate, but Abinadab isn't the one either.

> So, Jesse calls another of his fine, big sons. 'No,' Samuel tells him, 'God's not choosing him either.'

Well, by now, things are getting a little tense. And by the time seven of Jesse's sons have done the catwalk bit for Samuel and all been turned down flat – well, it's not looking hopeful. 'It's no good, Jesse,' Samuel says, 'you can pull all the faces you like, but God's not chosen any of these. Look, don't throw stones at me – I'm just the messenger.'

Stories for telling

Now, you must admit it all looks a bit suss. So, Samuel turns to Jesse again: 'You holding out on me or something? You trying to tell me these are all the sons you've got?'

Jesse looks embarrassed. 'Well, OK, there's one other – but he's just a kid – I mean the most useful thing he does is look after the sheep.' Jesse doesn't mention that David's a bit of a singer-songwriter – well, if you're spending all your time out on the hills counting sheep, you probably need a hobby to keep you awake.

'Well, don't just stand there, Jess – send for him!' Sam tells him. 'Unless, of course, you want to stand about here for ever.'

Jesse doesn't. So he does – send for David, that is. Samuel has to give him his due – he's a good-looking lad – a bit red in the face, perhaps, and definitely well on the small side. And he'll need more than those big, innocent-looking eyes to be a leader (well, you did in Samuel's day anyway). Samuel doesn't have long to think about it, because God's getting excited. 'That's the one! That's the one. Go on, Sammy, lad – get up and do it – anoint him – now!'

Well, what can Samuel do? He anoints him – right there, in front of all those strapping brothers of his: His Imperial Majesty, King David, the shepherd boy – has an odd kind of ring to it, doesn't it!

Well, there's only one thing any sensible prophet's going to do after that.

Samuel goes home.

He's the greatest – honest!

Crib sheet

Who was 'The Greatest'? (Ali)
Who was 'The King?' (Elvis)
God has other ways of measuring greatness – here's a story about a great king.

It begins when God decides he's had it with King Saul – impressive looking, but doesn't do things God's way. God tells Samuel to go to Jesse's place to anoint the next king.

Samuel: 'You must think I'm mad – he'll kill me!'
'Say you've come to conduct a service.'
Samuel goes to Jesse's – frightens local dignitaries – reassures Jesse.
First son: Eliab – looks good, but God looks at the heart – says no.
Next one – Abinadab – still no.

Seven sons paraded, but none of them is the one. Samuel: 'It's no good, Jesse, you can pull all the faces you like, but God's not chosen any of these. Look, don't throw stones at me – I'm just the messenger.'
One more – just a kid – looks after the sheep – oh, and he sings too.

Send for David – good-looking lad, but otherwise not impressive.
God gets excited: 'That's the one! That's the one. Go on, Sammy, lad – get up and do it – anoint him – now!'
So he does. Odd though: 'His Imperial Majesty, King David the shepherd boy'!
Only one thing left for Samuel to do: he goes home.

Power tends to corrupt

Based on 2 Samuel 11:1-27

Now, let's be fair: it's the sort of thing that can happen to anyone. There you are, walking around on your flat roof, when you just happen to look through someone's bathroom window. And they just happen to be taking a bath. As I said, it can happen to anyone – the important thing is what you do next. And that's where King David himself, no less – the greatest king the Israelites ever had – went and got it about as wrong as it gets.

> OK, so here's the scene. He's just taking a stroll on his roof when he looks across and down a bit, and – pow! What's he see? Only the most beautiful woman he's ever eyeballed in his life, in her bath, the altogether and blissful ignorance. And it's what he does next that gets him into terrible trouble. I mean, you or I – we'd have looked away, wouldn't we? Of course we would. David goes and gets his servants to find out who she is. Seriously, not a good idea.

And who is she? Only the wife of one of David's soldiers who's away at the war, that's all. And, she's all on her own. Even now, though, David's got time just to leave it at that – maybe recommend a good curtain fitter, but no more.

Now, I'm sure he thinks that it's all quite harmless when he invites her to the palace for dinner. I mean, if a king can't give a bit of hospitality to his soldiers' wives, what can he do? Well, let's just cut a long story short – I never was any good at bedroom scenes, anyway – and say that he offers a lot more than just hospitality.

Power tends to corrupt

So, you can guess what happens. Next thing we know, Bathsheba – did I tell you that was her name? – is coming round to tell David she's pregnant. Now, king or no king, David doesn't want Uriah – that's her husband – finding out about it. I mean, the guy's been away at the front for months, so he's bound to be, shall we say, suspicious? David knows he's got to hatch a cunning plot – and that's when he goes absolutely, completely OTT.

Now, be fair – bumping the husband off isn't actually his first option. 'Simple,' he thinks. 'Let's get Uriah back here for a spot of leave. He can spend a night or two at home with his wife, and with a little bit of luck he'll think the baby's his. So he sends for Uriah, asks him how the war's going and tells him to go home for a bit. And if Uriah had done that, he might have ended up a happier man – not to say actually alive.

But Uriah doesn't play ball. 'What, me, go home and spend the night with my wife,' he objects, 'when all my comrades are at the front fighting? No, it wouldn't be right.' So the guy ends up spending the night in Jerusalem but not going home.

Well, he's really cooked his goose now. David has only one other option left (apart from being honest and coming clean, of course, but since when did people in power choose to do things like that?) – and that's to kill Uriah. And to add insult to injury, he makes Uriah carry his own death warrant back to the front. It's a letter from King David to the general, Joab. 'Put Uriah in the front line,' it says, 'and then when he's surrounded by enemies, pull back.' I mean, can you imagine the complacency – sending that letter by the very man he's trying to get killed? Now, is that an abuse of trust, or what?

Now, the trouble with that kind of tactic is that it's a blunt instrument – you can hardly expect to predict who else may get killed. So it is that a number of soldiers die in the

Stories for telling

battle, including Uriah. Oh, he puts up a good fight, of course – he's a brave guy, and he thinks he's fighting for a king who's worth dying for. There again, he's not the first or the last person in history to make *that* mistake either.

The one I feel sorry for is the poor messenger who has to go and tell Bathsheba that her husband's dead. OK, so she might be having a fling with the king, but that doesn't mean she doesn't still love the guy, does it? So she goes into deep mourning – while the king bides his time.

> Then the official mourning period comes to an end, and David makes his move. He brings her to his house, sets her up as his own wife, and she has their son. They seem to think that that's all there is to it: he's happy, she's happy, the baby, of course, has no idea about anything, and the whole country's none the wiser.

But there is someone who knows – and who's not just going to let sleeping dogs lie. And that someone is . . . My word – is that the time? I'll have to tell you the rest another day.

Power tends to corrupt

Crib sheet

The sort of thing that can happen to anyone: walking around on the roof – look down – see someone taking a bath.

Important point: what you do next! That's where King David went wrong.

So, there he is, just strolling on the roof – beautiful woman in bath. We'd look away – he doesn't. Finds out who she is: wife of soldier away at war.

Invites her round . . . do I have to spell it out? Soon, Bathsheba (did I tell you that was her name?) is coming round to say she's pregnant.

Uriah (husband) has been at the front for months – he'll know it's not his.

David gives Uriah leave – Uriah refuses to go home – only two options left: come clean or lose Uriah.

Sends Uriah back with note for commander: leave him exposed to danger.

Several unnecessary deaths – including Uriah's – they think they're dying in a good cause!

Messenger goes to Bathsheba – straight into mourning – David bides his time.

Mourning over – Bathsheba becomes David's wife – has their son. They've hushed it all up successfully – they think . . .

But someone knows. Gosh – that the time?

Tell you the rest another day.

The game's up, David

Based on 2 Samuel 11:26-12:13a

Have you ever done something you hope no one finds out about? I'm not talking about the scandal of the millennium here – it could be just something that's a bit embarrassing – you know, something that dents the carefully polished image and shows you're not perfect. There again, of course, it might be the scandal of the millennium – in which case I'd really rather not know, anyway.

That's how it is for King David as we find him at the beginning of this story. He's committed adultery and covered it up with a multiple murder. Now, it's not that I want to shatter your illusions or anything, but right now the writer of the twenty-third Psalm is not quite the role model we'd all like to think. In fact, at this moment he's well guilty!

Of course, he thinks he's OK, because no one knows. But he's wrong – because Someone knows. Someone with a big, big, capital S knows – or should that be capital G? And he's not likely to let it lie – there's been enough lying already, thank you very much. So God's had a word with Nathan the prophet, and Nathan's on his way round to see David.

Nathan knows he's got to box clever on this one – I mean, when the Main Man's gone seriously off the rails, you don't just walk up and tell him so – but Nathan's a wily old ferret and he knows he's got to get David on his side.

'I've got something to tell you,' he says to him. 'It's about an injustice – and as you're the king you're just the guy to deal with it.' Nothing like appealing to someone's pride,

The game's up, David

you see. Then he goes on. 'There are these two men, see: one rich and one poor. Now the rich man – well, he's just loaded with sheep, lambs, goats, you name it. The poor guy's just got one little lamb. He bought it out of his own savings – brought it up like a child – treats it like one of the family. I mean, he even lets it eat and drink from the same plates and cups – not my idea of health and hygiene, but each to his own, I say. Put it simply: the lamb's like his own little baby girl.'

> Nathan can see he's got King David well hooked. Sheep, see – he might be king but he's never forgotten about shepherding, and he knows how attached you can get. So Nathan moves in for the kill.

'Well, Your Majesty, the rich man has a visitor, and he's got to feed him. No problem, you might think – he's got animals all over the hillside, so he's not going to miss one, now is he? Would you believe that he goes and steals his neighbour's little lamb? Honest – goes right in there, whips it from right under his nose and serves it up with mint sauce and a nice thyme and parsley stuffing.'

> Nathan's done a good job with this – really got King David fired up. David's spitting radioactive fallout. 'Lead me to him!' he's yelling. 'As sure as there's a God in heaven, this guy's vulture-fodder – but not before he's paid back four times what he stole. Of all the uncaring, pitiless, heartless, subhuman, totally unforgivable . . . well, I'm speechless!'

'I'm glad you feel like that, Your Majesty,' Nathan said. 'Because it's you – you're the bad guy in this story. Now, close your mouth, put your eyes back in their sockets and listen to what God says. "I made you king of Israel," he says. "Without me, you'd be nothing. Didn't I save you from Saul when he was after having your blood in a bottle? Didn't I let you take over his house – not to mention his harem, which should have been quite enough for any guy to handle? Didn't I give you not only Israel to rule over but

Stories for telling

Judah as well – I mean, correct me if I'm missing something, here, but did I ever keep you short? And even if I had, you only had to ask for more! So, why've you treated my word with less respect than a tabloid journalist (don't try and work it out, they're after your time)? Why've you flown against everything I stand for? Oh, don't put on that innocent expression with me – I know all about what you did to Uriah the Hittite – and what you got up to with his wife, if it comes to that. Well, what's sauce for the goose is sage and onion for the rooster, so you won't be surprised if others start treating *you* like that, will you? I mean, if the king can't be trusted, why should his subjects be any different? You don't respect them – why should they respect you? You've blown it, old lad – and you might have been discreet, but no one's going to hide it when it happens to you. Take my word for it, you'll be well humiliated. You've had the forbidden fruit – here's your just deserts.'"

Well, to give David his due, he knows how to admit when he's wrong. 'You're right,' he says, 'I've really messed up – big time.' Now, I don't know about you, but I reckon it's precisely that that makes him a great king. I reckon there are a few people around right now who could learn from this guy.

The game's up, David

Crib sheet

We all have embarrassing secrets.

King David's got a really bad one: adultery, murder – not quite the role model we like to think he is!

Thinks no one knows, but Someone does – and God's told Nathan to confront David.

> Nathan – got to get David on his side.
>
> Appeals to David's pride – champion of justice.
>
> Two men, one rich (huge flocks) one poor (one beloved lamb).
>
> Rich man has visitor – steals poor man's lamb to serve to him, with seasoning, for dinner.

David falls for it: 'He's dead!'

Nathan: 'It's you!'

Hear what God says: 'After all I've given you:
- kingship
- Saul's house and harem
- Israel and Judah

> 'Not enough? Only had to ask for more.
>
> 'Why treat my word with disrespect?
>
> 'I know all about Uriah and Bathsheba.
>
> 'You play dirty – you get dirty yourself. Don't expect to be treated any better.'

David admits he's wrong – *that's* what makes him a great king.

A few people today could learn that from him!

Elijah and the widow

Based on 1 Kings 17:1-16

I'd like to tell you about one of God's prophets – a guy called Elijah. As we meet him, he's in a spot of bother – as a matter of fact, he's usually in spots of bother. You might say that spots of bother are familiar territory to Elijah. It's a lifestyle thing: Elijah doesn't approve of the lifestyle of the king and queen – well, to be more accurate, he knows that *God* doesn't approve of it – and he just won't stop saying so.

> The king's called Ahab – and he's one of the most ungodly monarchs ever to park his bottom on the throne of Israel. The queen? Well, that's dear old Queen Jezebel. You've heard people described as bad news? Well, Jezebel's the whole bulletin. I mean, if she were alive now, the BBC wouldn't put her on until after the watershed, and even then only with a warning message.

Now, you mustn't let me get carried away here – I could spend all the time we've got telling you horror stories about Ahab and Jezebel, but it's really Elijah we're concerned with now.

Elijah's got himself into real strife, telling the king and queen what God thinks of the way they live. He won't leave the subject alone – goes on and on about it, he does – on and on and on – just won't stop – on and on and on and on – he won't give up going on and on and on . . . and, as you've just been thinking, it gets a bit wearing after a while.

> Jezebel's well angry, and when Jezebel's angry, Ahab is too – if he knows what's good for him. Did I tell you they were the worst king and queen ever? Just checking.

Elijah and the widow

> Anyway, let's get on with the story. Elijah's just told Ahab and Jezebel that there's going to be a famine – and a drought too – and they're reacting in just the way you'd expect: if you don't like the message – kill the messenger.

Now, God knows it's no good pointing out to them that killing Elijah won't make it rain – so he decides to get Elijah away for a bit until the heat dies down. 'Go east, young man,' he tells him. 'First stop is the stream at Cherith. You can drink from the water, and I've arranged for your food to be flown in.'

'Flown in?' Now, Elijah might be a great prophet, but aeroplanes are a bit ambitious for even him to know about. Anyway, don't get your hopes up: God's got the sense to know that the simplest solutions are the best. And that means ravens – flocks of them – doing two drops a day of bread and meat to keep Elijah alive.

> It's clever stuff, but it can't last: there's a drought, remember? The stream dries up, and Elijah's got to move. 'OK, so go to Zarephath,' God tells him. 'There's a widow there who'll give you food and water.' So Elijah picks up his spirits, his feet and his backpack and sets off for Zarephath. And right there, at the town gate, is a woman collecting bits of wood for a fire.

'Hey, lady,' Elijah calls, 'You got a bit of water to spare for me?' Now, believe it or believe it not, she just goes off to fetch some – just like that – for a complete stranger! So Elijah decides to go the whole hog. 'How's about a bit of bread?' he says.

The woman stops, and turns round. 'You're pushing your luck, you are!' she says. 'Look, I'm telling you, as sure as there's a God in heaven, I've got just enough flour and oil for my boy and me to have a last meal before we die. Give you some, too? Somehow, I think not – know what I mean?'

'Oh, don't worry about that!' Elijah tells her. 'Look, here's

Stories for telling

the deal: you do this for me, and I'll tell you what God's saying. He's saying that your flour jar will never be empty – and your oil will never run dry. You'll be provided for until the drought ends. That's 'cos I'm a prophet, see: you look after me – God'll take care of you.'

Now, remember, Elijah's already been living rough for quite a while. The widow looks him up and down, from his tangled hair, down past his smelly tunic to his grimy, gritty and gently steaming feet. She could say that if this is God's idea of taking care of someone she'll settle for that last meal, thank you very much – but for some reason she believes him. So off she goes and makes up the dough for Elijah's cake.

> Well, what do you know? It only works out exactly as Elijah says, that's all! The flour jar always seems to have flour in it, and the oil flask never runs dry – exactly as Elijah told her God had promised.

Now, you may be wondering what's happened to King Ahab and Queen Jezebel. Oh, I don't think I told you that they're the worst, most evil, most horrifyingly obnoxious king and queen ever. I did? Well, now I've told you again. I mean, I could go on and on about them for ages – oh, I've done that bit too, have I?

Well, anyway, they're still around – still bad news – and Elijah hasn't finished with them yet.

Elijah and the widow

Crib sheet

One of God's prophets – Elijah – in a spot of bother.

Criticises king and queen – Ahab and Jezebel – they're bad news.

> I could easily go on about Ahab and Jezebel, but Elijah's our subject.

Keeps denouncing king and queen's lifestyle: on and on . . . they're fed up with it.

Jezebel's angry – that means Ahab is, too. Elijah's just prophesied famine and drought.

> God sends Elijah east – live near a brook, food will be airlifted in.
>
> Stream dries up – God sends Elijah to Zarephath.

Widow at town gate gathering sticks. Elijah asks for water.

Then asks for cake – no chance – last family meal coming up.

God's promise: do this and you'll never run out.

> (Elijah hardly looks as if God's cared for him!)

For some reason, she believes him – turns out as promised.

So, what of Ahab and Jezebel?

Still around – still bad news – Elijah hasn't finished with them yet.

You're never alone

Based on 1 Kings 19:9-18

Do you ever get the idea that you're the only one who understands? Everyone else has got it completely wrong – you're the only one who's still got a grip on reality? It's an occupational hazard for us religious types, I'm afraid. And just to show that it happens to the best of us, take poor old Elijah.

Now, don't get me wrong: Elijah's not suffering from paranoia – they really are out to get him. By 'they' I mean King Ahab and Queen Jezebel – well, Queen Jezebel mainly, but King Ahab knows better than to argue with her, which is where he seems to be a bit wiser than Elijah. Elijah's lit the blue touch paper in no uncertain terms, and now he's having to move faster than a rumour in a congregation in order to get to a safe distance.

That's how he wound up in this cave, where he thought nobody was ever going to find him. No *body* is about right – but God isn't hampered by one of those, so he's kept up with Elijah all the way. And now, it's time for a chat. So Elijah's hardly begun to catch his breath when he has to do a sharp intake of the same stuff.

'Hi, Elijah – what brings you to a place like this?'

Well, Elijah may be scared, but he's not completely lost it; he recognises God's voice straight away.

'"What am I doing here?"' he echoes. 'Do you know what it's like out there? I mean, seriously, do you? I'm the best friend you've got – I've been right there standing up for you, defending your interests, all that stuff. Everybody

You're never alone

else – well, they've really let you down: wrecked all your worship centres, slaughtered your best men – except me, of course – I'm the only one left and now they're out to get me too.'

God's not impressed. 'Yeah, yeah, yeah, I know – all the usual stuff. Look, Elijah: go and stand at the entrance to the cave, because I'm going to make myself known to you and you might just learn something.'

> This is too good a chance to miss, so Elijah goes to the cave entrance and peers out. Not for long, though – he's almost blown back into the cave by the wind. This is a wind like nothing else you've ever known: huge trees flying past as if they're made of paper, giant boulders rising into the slipstream and breaking up with the pressure – but it's when the mountains start crumbling around him that, well, Elijah just sort of knows that this is something a bit different. Strange thing, though: God's not in the wind.

Elijah's only just starting to think about that when the wind stops. That's better. Now it's just an earthquake: the whole mountain range heaving and rumbling like an enormous, oversensitive stomach after a strong curry – but God's not in that, either. And that's when the fire hits: I tell you, Steven Spielberg couldn't recreate this, not in a million years. Elijah's never seen flames or felt heat like it. And still no sign of God.

> And then – after the wind, and the earthquake and the fire – the most terrifying experience Elijah's ever had in his life: silence. A deep, dark, all-consuming silence – not so much an absence of noise as the overwhelming of it by something infinitely more powerful. It's awesome – absolutely awesome. Elijah wraps his cloak around his head and forces his trembling feet back to the mouth of the cave. And that's when he hears it: from the very bowels of the silence, a soft, haunting voice asks, 'What are you doing here, Elijah?'

Stories for telling

Elijah starts babbling again: 'Me? I'm on your side. I've been really good – you know – really enthusiastic? I mean, not like all those other so-called Israelites – knocking down your altars, killing your prophets – I'm the only one left, and now they're after me too.'

God's heard all this before, of course. 'Oh, get away!' he says. 'No, seriously, Elijah – you need to get away. Go to the Damascus desert – and while you're there you can start anointing new kings and prophets. They'll take care of the troublemakers, don't you worry. Oh, and as for all this "I'm the only one who's got it right" stuff, well, let's just say you'll find there are more of you than you think. Seven thousand of them. That's right, seven thousand – I don't make mistakes where arithmetic's concerned: it's one of my strong subjects. And talking of strong subjects, you'll find that that's exactly what these people are – all seven thousand of them, strong subjects of mine. Now, go, Elijah.'

So, Elijah goes – and guess what? It turns out that God's absolutely right.

Which is no surprise, really, is it?

Crib sheet

Ever think only you are right? Occupational hazard for religious types. Take poor Elijah:

King Ahab and Queen Jezebel out to get him – he's been playing with fire and now on the run.

Ends up in a cave – only God's still with him:

> 'What are you doing here, Elijah?'
>
> 'I'm your only friend – altars wrecked, prophets killed, etc – only me left and they're after me too.'

'Go to cave entrance: I'll meet you there.'
- wind
- earthquake
- fire
- terrible, awesome silence

> Whisper: same question and answer.

'Get away! To desert near Damascus – anoint kings and prophets. 7,000 faithful, strong subjects still around. Just go!'

God's right. Not surprising!

The God-given right to do wrong?
Based on 1 Kings 21:1-24

It's a sad fact that when people get too much power they tend to start thinking they've got a divine right to get what they want – especially if it belongs to someone weaker than themselves. That's the same whether we're talking about kings, prime ministers, presidents or business big-shots. And just to show that it's nothing new, here's a story from the Bible about it.

We're talking King Ahab and Queen Jezebel here – two of the most despicable despots you can think of. Well, she is, anyway – he's just pathetic, but when you're married to a Jezebel, that's just as dangerous.

So, anyway, King Ahab pops down the palace garden to have a word with Naboth, his next-door neighbour. 'Nice bit of land, this,' he says. 'I want it.'

'Oh, you do, do you?' Naboth answers. Then he leans on his hoe and looks thoughtful. 'Now, my old nanny always told me that "I want" doesn't get. So, I'll tell you what. You ask nicely, and I'll consider it.'

Ahab thinks for a moment – it takes time for things like that to get through when you're more accustomed to tugged forelocks and unquestioning compliance. 'OK, OK,' he sighs. 'Can I have your land, *please*?'

'That's better,' Naboth answers. 'Now, let me think . . . No.'

Ahab just gapes at him. 'No?'

'No!' Naboth repeats. 'Sorry, is that too equivocal for you?

The God-given right to do wrong?

> Let me try and make it clearer. Negative. Absolutely out of the question. This was my father's land before it was mine – been in the family for centuries, it has, but then what would you know about the value of history? It'd be unthinkable to sell it to you, and I'm not going to. Now, is there anything there that needs to be explained, or do you think you understand it now?'

Well, now Ahab's in a right old state. I mean, if he doesn't expand his property, what's he going to do with all these little bushes that are springing up everywhere? So, he does what diplomats of his calibre always do when they can't get their own way: he goes away and sulks.

That's where Queen Jezebel finds him: lying on his bed, with his face to the wall, with a scowl on it that could turn milk to Gorgonzola.

> Jezebel's not pleased when she hears that Naboth's refused to let Ahab have his land. After all, who does Naboth think he is? I mean, does he really think that having that tin-pot bit of land gives him the right to decide what to do with it? Doesn't he understand the politics of power? 'Don't worry,' she soothes Ahab. 'That land's as good as yours. Now, get up, wipe your eyes and do try to look like the world leader you're supposed to be.' Then she goes off to write some letters.

The next thing Naboth knows about it, he's up in court accused of blasphemy. Not that he's too worried at first, because he thinks the Security Council will give him a fair hearing. Unfortunately, Ahab and Jezebel have got some little friends with big ideas who want to keep on the right side of them – and they'll say anything to do that. So they end up persuading the court to do what Jezebel wants, and poor old Naboth's got all the big guns lined up against him. Of course, he carries on protesting about the injustice of it all, but he knows there's no point. The People With Power have decided they want to take over his land, and all the

Stories for telling

others know which is the winning side and are falling over themselves to be on it.

So it is that Naboth gets stoned. And by that, I don't mean that he goes out and drowns his sorrows. Stoning to death is the standard punishment for blasphemy, and it fits Jezebel's purpose because someone who's stoned to death can't defend themselves.

After it's all over, Jezebel goes to Ahab and says, 'He's gone – dead – defunct – no more problems from that little man. The land's all yours to do as you like with – and the best bit is it's all legal. Well, it looks it, anyway.'

So, Ahab goes down to the garden and walks in – because there's no one there to stop him now. 'It's mine!' he says. 'All mine! Now, is that power or is that power!'

> But hang on – who's this coming? Elijah, the prophet. Soon as he sees him, Ahab's scared, so he gets aggressive. 'Enemy!' he shrieks. 'Enemy! I know you're my enemy because, as I always say, "You're either with me or against me" – and I just know you're not with me. Enemy within! Enemy within!'
>
> Elijah hasn't got time for all this. 'Oh, do shut up and listen!' he says. 'Save all that stuff for the speeches – it doesn't impress me at all. I'm just here to tell you that you're going to wish you'd never messed with Naboth. You want to play dirty? Well, that's your choice, but if you do, then you can't complain when others play dirty with you.'

I think that's the place to leave that conversation because it gets a bit gruesome. Suffice to say that Ahab and Jezebel don't listen – their sort never do – and everything Elijah said comes true.

You see, the big mistake they made was thinking that God was on their side just because they'd got the power. They never got their heads round the fact that God isn't on the side of power – he's on the side of justice.

The God-given right to do wrong?

Crib sheet

Too much power = delusions of 'divine rights' – especially over people who are weaker.

Queen Jezebel and King Ahab – despotic and pathetic respectively.

Ahab tells Naboth, 'I want your land' – gets short shrift.

Ahab sulks – Jezebel comforts him and promises to get him what he wants.

Jezebel writes letters: Naboth falsely accused of blasphemy and found guilty on false testimony.

Naboth stoned to death – Jezebel 'gives' his garden to Ahab.

Before he can celebrate, Elijah the prophet arrives. Ahab panics: 'Enemy!'

Elijah: 'You play dirty with others, you can't be surprised if they play dirty with you.' Goes on to forecast things too gruesome for this page!

It all comes true. Big mistake: thinking God's on the side of power – he's on the side of justice.

Oh, just do it!

Based on 2 Kings 5:1-14

Let me tell you about a guy called Naaman. Real big-shot – Commander-in-Chief of the entire army of the king of Aram. Now, you may not think Aram's exactly a world power, but just a few thousand years ago – which is when we're talking about – you only had to mention its name to get politicians' knees knocking.

Now, being a big-shot is OK, as long as you can look the part. And that's where Naaman's got a problem. His skin looks like someone's been at it with a cheese-grater. All over his body, he's like that, and it really is a horrible way to be. So of course he wants to get shot of the problem – quickly.

Now, as it happens, he's got a slave girl – an Israelite, captured on a raid or some such enterprise – and although you might think she's got good reason not to like Naaman, she wouldn't wish his problem on anybody at all. So one day she has a quiet word with his wife.

'Look,' she says, 'I know he thinks my people are inferior and all that, but he really ought to go and see the prophet in Samaria – real holy man, he is – he'd sort him out.'

Well, the wife tells Naaman, and Naaman tells the king, and in less time than it takes to say, 'What, me, ask an Israelite for a favour?' the king of Aram's written a letter to the king of Israel, doing just that.

So, there's the king of Israel, with a letter from his worst enemy saying, 'I want you to cure my Commander-in-Chief

Oh, just do it!

of his skin disease.' How would you feel? I mean, see it from his point of view – it's obviously a trap, isn't it?

'I know his game!' he says. 'Does he really think I'd be in politics if I could solve people's problems? He's picking a fight, that's what. He wants me to try, and then when I fail he'll send an army to get revenge. *Now* what am I going to do?'

So, now we've got Naaman tearing his hair out, the king of Israel tearing his clothes, and a battery of diplomats tearing around looking for the right way to say, 'Get lost'!

> Which is all rather unnecessary, because there *is* someone who can do it. Elisha, his name is, and he's a prophet. He's got all the kit – tatty clothes, long beard, gleam in his eye – and he reckons it's time the Aramaeans found out where the real power is. 'There, there, kingy-fellow,' he says, 'don't go tearing up those lovely royal threads – just send this character to me. I'll show him that there's a real prophet in Israel.'

Next thing anyone knows, Elisha's neighbours think they're the location for a John Wayne movie: horses, chariots and the entire Aramaean version of the Ninth Cavalry. And all for little old Naaman and his itchy epidermis! Naaman gets out of his chariot, struts down the path and knocks on Elisha's door, but Elisha's not impressed by it all. The door opens and it's Elisha's servant. 'Oh, it's you,' he says, as if Syrian chiefs of staff parade outside asking for favours every day. 'Go and have a wash! Well, actually, have seven washes – you'll find the River Jordan just over there: straight down between the butcher's and the baker's, left at "Candlesticks R Us" and you can't miss it. Bye.' And the door closes.

> Now, that's not how anyone speaks to the guy who calls the shots in the world's most powerful army. Except that someone just has. So Naaman does what people in his position usually do when they get humiliated – takes it out on someone else, in this case his own servant. 'What's he mean,

Stories for telling

> "Go and wash"!' he rants. 'He's supposed to come and do something spectacular: use the magic words and wave his magic wand – well, pray to his God and wave his hand, at the very least – and just wave the problem away. Isn't that what holy people do? I mean, if I've *really* got to wash, I can do that at home in Damascus – in the River Abana, or in the Pharpar. They're better than the mouldy old Jordan, any day.' And he's storming off back to his chariot in a rage like no one's ever raged before.

Luckily, as is often the case with such people, his servants have more sense than he has, and they try to calm him down. 'Look, boss,' they say, 'what's your problem? Too easy for you, is it? Beneath your dignity? I mean, if he'd asked you to do something really impressive – something difficult or dangerous – oh, yes, you'd have done that, wouldn't you! So why not just go and wash – not a lot to ask.'

> So that's how we find Naaman, the great Commander-in-Chief of an all-conquering army, taking all his clothes off and wading into the Jordan. He grits his teeth and goes under – comes up spluttering, snorting and still itching. 'Seven times' was what the guy said. Oh, well – may as well do it. Six more times, he goes under that water – with all his junior officers and other ranks standing there watching. Then he comes up for the seventh time.

Suddenly, everyone stops staring and starts gawping: look, no more pizza topping – just smooth, clear, perfect skin like a child's. Now, that might be embarrassing for a rough, tough, fighting man, but at least it doesn't make everyone avoid him.

Just goes to show: sometimes it's the little tasks – the ones with no glory in them – that turn out to have the impressive results.

Oh, just do it!

Crib sheet

Naaman – real big-shot – Commander-in-Chief of Aramaean army.

Doesn't look the part – skin like grated cheese.

Slave girl (captured Israelite) says he should go to prophet in Samaria.

King of Aram writes to king of Israel – who thinks he's trying to pick a quarrel.

Elisha – good, old fashioned hairy prophet – says, 'Send him to me.'

Naaman arrives – with entourage. Elisha sends message by servant – go and wash in the Jordan seven times.

Naaman's not impressed – insulted, in fact. Why not wash in River Abana or Pharpar at Damascus?

Servants: 'What's wrong – not difficult/impressive enough for you?'

So he does – seven dips in the Jordan.

No more pizza topping – skin like a child's.

Sometimes it's the little things we do that count.

New life for old bones
Based on Ezekiel 37:1-14

You know, the trouble with God is he's unpredictable – you never know what he's going to think of doing next. I mean, there I am, sitting in my garden, enjoying a nice juicy pomegranate and minding my own business like any good religious person, when suddenly I'm not there any more.

The hand of God – that's what it is, and no mistake – picks me up, whisks me off into the blue, and puts me down in the most bizarre place you've ever seen. And fast? I've never moved like it – not even time to watch the in-flight movie on the way.

So, there I am, standing on the side of a hill looking across a valley. I don't mind telling you, I don't ever want to go there again – it's well spooky. There's nothing but bones, as far as the eye can see. And I'm talking human remains here, not your regular everyday doggie treats. All kinds, there are: skulls, shin bones, fingers, toes, and all as dry as – oh, I see, so that's where that saying comes from! Well, anyway, I don't know what happened in this place, but I want out before I get it, too.

Then there's this voice: 'Hey, there, little mortal person – what do you reckon – can these bones have life again?'

Well, I know who the voice is, of course – it's got to be God, because no one else would come to a place like this. Has he dragged me all the way out here – wherever I am – just to ask me that? 'Look, God,' I say to him, 'you're the only one who can answer that.'

New life for old bones

'Fair enough,' he says, 'but it isn't that simple. I want *you* to do it. Prophesy – go on, it's what you do, isn't it – prophesy to these old dry bones.' And he goes on to tell me exactly what to say.

So there I am, feeling like a complete banana-brain, in a place I don't know, with no idea how I got there, talking to a load of old bones. It's enough to make you lose confidence in your own sanity. 'Now, listen up, you bones,' I say to them. 'Listen to what God says: I'm going to put breath back into you, and you're going to live. You'll have flesh, muscles, skin, breath – the whole works. That'll show you who's God around here.'

Suddenly, there's such a rattling as you've never heard, as all those bones start to get together. There are fingers beckoning to each other, vertebrae jumping on each other's shoulders like circus acrobats, and the air's thick with skulls whizzing round looking for spines to land on. Laugh? I tell you, you've never seen a sight like a pair of legs chasing around the hillside looking for a pelvic girdle.

But then it gets gruesome. Suddenly, they all start growing flesh. Gross? You don't know the half of it – enough to make you turn veggie on the spot. When the skin's finished, they look better – but that doesn't stop me getting flashbacks for years afterwards. Trouble is, though, they're still dead – not enough breath between them to blow out a match.

Then, the Voice starts up again. 'Well, don't just stand there, little mortal person – prophesy again. Say, "Listen to the word of God, you breath: come from the four winds and fill these here dead folks, so that they can live."'

Have you ever felt the wind coming from four different directions at once? No? Well, just pray it stays that way. There's only one thing to do: grit your teeth and wait till it's over. And when it's over, it isn't over – I'm still there, and I'm looking at a mass of people, all living and breathing

Stories for telling

like it's a new craze or something. And there're thousands of them. God alone knows how they're going to explain this to the Department of Census and Population Control.

I don't get much time to wonder about that, though, because God's bending my ear again. 'Now, get this, little mortal person: think of these bones as the nation, right? Just like a load of old dry bones, they are. Well, you go and prophesy to them. Say, "This is what God says: time to wake up and get out of those graves you call your lives, because I'm going to open them up like a wine bottle at a party, and you're going to come bubbling out. I'm going to give you my own spirit, that's what – and put you back where you belong. Then you're going to know who's really God around this place!"'

And, do you know, I really believe he means it. I don't know whether to be excited or scared stiff!

Crib sheet

Trouble with God – unpredictable.

Suddenly I'm in the most bizarre valley.

It's well spooky – bones – human ones.

God speaks: Can these bones live?

'Prophesy to the bones' – so I do.

Rattling – bones come together – rushing all over the place, pairing up.

Then it gets gruesome – flesh, etc. – gross! Then skin – that's better – but they're still dead.

God again: prophesy to the breath – call the four winds.

Suddenly, they're all alive – thousands of them!

God: bones are the nation – prophesy new life for the nation.

I think he means it – don't know whether to be excited or scared stiff!

You can run but you can't hide

Based on Jonah 1-2

I'm going to tell you the story of Jonah. Now, he's actually not a bad sort of guy – probably feeds his cat regularly, raises his hat to ladies in the street, all that kind of thing – because you don't need to be a bad person to be prejudiced. And, boy, is Jonah prejudiced! Which is how he gets to be in a very nasty situation.

It all begins one morning, about, oh, maybe two and a half thousand years ago – nobody knows, exactly, but it was before I was born, anyway – when God has one of his bright ideas. 'I'll send Jonah to Nineveh,' he thinks. 'Travel will broaden his mind – and it's well in need of broadening.' Jonah's not impressed.

'Oh, I know your game,' he says. 'You want me to go and preach to those lousy, rotten people, don't you! Well, I'm not up for it, and that's that. It'll be the old, old story – they'll repent, you'll forgive them, and they won't get theirs.'

Still, Jonah knows it's no good arguing with God – so he decides to get away. And that's how he ends up down at the docks at Joppa, looking for a ship to Spain. 'So, God wants me to travel, does he?' he's thinking. ''Well, I'll go and hide away for a bit.'

Now, I've heard some bad ideas in my time, but trying to hide where God can't find you is *well* ridiculous. And I suppose God could just have a quite word in Jonah's ear to point that out and save him a lot of trouble – but Jonah probably

> wouldn't listen, and anyway it wouldn't be half as good a story. So Jonah gets on the ship, pays his fare and starts dreaming of sand, sea and a God-free environment.

Life, of course, is never that simple. God decides it's time Jonah found out that there's nowhere that God isn't. Absolutely nowhere. And stage one of the plan is to cook up a nice, juicy storm. Soon, the waves are throwing the boat up and down like a bag-full of bungee jumpers. It's completely manic – up, down, back up again, meeting your stomach on its way down. And let's hope you enjoyed your last meal, because you're going to get to experience it all over again from a different angle.

> By now the sailors have tried everything: they've prayed to more gods than they ever believed in to start with; they've thrown all the baggage overboard to lighten the ship – but that just makes it easier for the sea to throw up (if you'll forgive the expression) and down. And where's Jonah all this time? Down in the ship's hold, absolutely fast asleep. I mean, is he insensitive or what? He's in for a rude awakening. Run away from God? He can't even hide from the ship's captain.

Even I'm not going to repeat the captain's exact words – let's just say that 'Get off your butt and start praying to your God, you idle little parasite' is the polite version. Meanwhile, the sailors are getting really scientific – drawing lots to see whose fault it all is! OK, but let's remember this was thousands of years ago, and be fair – there are still people believing this kind of stuff now! Anyway, as it happens, it works and they all start pointing fingers at Jonah.

'Who are you?' they're asking. 'Where are you from? What's your tribe?'

Well, this is definitely not the time for smart-alec answers like, 'Manchester United', so Jonah just says, 'I'm a Hebrew, actually. I worship the God who made all this stuff – you know, land, sea, little green apples, the works.' Oh,

Stories for telling

yes, and at some point he lets it slip that he's running away from God. Nice one, Jonah!

> Well, that decides it. After that, everyone knows that every bad thing, from rain on bank holidays to the Mesopotamian national debt, is Jonah's fault. The problem is, what are they going to do about it? Not an easy question to answer when the floor you're standing on is dancing a hornpipe, and your brain won't stay still long enough to make contact.

Anyway, to cut a long story short, Jonah does the decent thing at last, and volunteers to be slung over the side because he knows that'll induce God to stop making waves in the bath. Well, they don't want to do it – and they keep trying to steer the boat, but the end's predictable. Over the side Jonah goes, and the storm ends just like that and all the sailors decide God's the one for them and start worshipping. OK?

Oh, sorry – I'd forgotten Jonah for a minute. Well, luckily, God hasn't – he's got something really special lined up. How does a big fish grab you? If you're careful, it doesn't – but Jonah's too late for that. Have you any idea what it's like to be swallowed? I mean, getting past the mouth's the easy bit. Past the tonsils, into the gullet, and then comes the big squeeze – on and on he goes, passed from one vice-like set of muscles to another, and all the time it's getting darker and wetter, and stickier and smellier, until he finishes up in a stomach the size of Fingal's cave. And can you imagine what else might be in there? I mean do you have any idea what sort of stuff you'd find in a sea-monster's stomach?

> OK, so what now? Well, there's a couple of choices, but neither really bears thinking about. So, when all else fails: pray. And, boy, does Jonah pray! 'Oh, thank you, God, for saving me!' he grovels. 'OK, then, I'll do it. Whatever you want. Just name it – OK?'

Well, that's the short version. The original goes on a bit longer. Three days, Jonah was in that place: three days to think, to cry, to pray, before eventually the fish threw Jonah up on to dry land. And if you think getting *in* was bad . . .

Anyway, Jonah learns his lesson. I mean, if God could hear his prayers from the inside of a fish at fifty fathoms, well, there really is no hiding place – is there!

Stories for telling

Crib sheet

Jonah – nice guy, but prejudiced. God wants him to preach at Nineveh – but Jonah doesn't want foreigners to be saved.

No good arguing with God – Jonah finds a ship to Spain, to hide away. Bad idea.

Jonah boards ship – settles down – God decides it's time to teach him about omnipresence.

Storm – like bungee-jumping.

Jonah's asleep – captain wakes him: 'Get off your butt and pray!'

Sailors draw lots – blame lands on Jonah. 'Who are you? What tribe?'

Jonah: 'I worship the God who made all this.' Lets slip he's on the run. Now they *know* it's his fault!

Jonah volunteers as the fall guy – storm stops – sailors worship God. But what about Jonah?

How does a big fish grab you? Describe Jonah's unpleasant journey. Jonah's in the fish's stomach – what else might be in there?

No good choices – time to pray! 'Thanks . . . and . . . whatever it is, I'll do it'!

Jonah learns his lesson: if God could hear his prayers from the inside of a fish at fifty fathoms, well, there really is no hiding place – is there!

God shows who really counts
Based on Luke 2:1-20

Now, you'd think the ruler of the biggest empire in the world would have better things to do than count people – wouldn't you? Mind you, seeing the things that some modern leaders get up to, it might be better if that was all they did – but that's another issue.

Perhaps things were less complicated two thousand years ago, in ancient Rome, I don't know – but anyway, there sits Emperor Augustus Caesar on his throne, wondering how to pass the time, and he thinks, 'Oh, I know – I'll do what politicians always do – I'll find work for other people.' And next thing anyone knows, there's a massive census going on, and everyone's got to go back to the place they were born, to be counted.

And that's how Joseph and Mary come to be on the Bethlehem trail, just at the time when she should be taking it easy – a woman in her condition and all that. Well, even if the baby hadn't been due, the journey would probably have been enough to give it rather more than a nudge. Anyway, there they are in Bethlehem, with a new baby, and all they've got for a cradle is a feeding trough full of hay for the cattle. Well, it seems there's no room for Mary in the guest room.

Meanwhile, out on the hills, minding their own business and a flock of sheep, are some shepherds. Just ordinary shepherds, wondering how they're going to pass the time until dawn when suddenly it's brighter than Blackpool in October. The reason it's light is that an angel's come to

Stories for telling

visit, and brought the light of God's own glory with him – so who'd want Blackpool, anyway, when they can have that?

Terrified? I'd say so! Well, it's not your average everyday event, now, is it? Or every-night event, for that matter. But the angel reassures them. 'Hey, chill out, you guys,' he says. 'I've come to bring some good news – and it's just for you! Well, you and the rest of the world, actually, but you're the ones who're being told about it. It's your Saviour – he's here – in the city of David actually – born this very day, so this is really hot news. Anyway, I'll tell you how to recognise him – he's wrapped up in swaddling clothes, and he's lying in a cattle feeding trough – so you're not likely to find two of those in the same postal district.'

The angel's no sooner finished talking than God really turns on the pyrotechnics – and there's never been a royal fireworks display like this one, I can tell you. Lights, music and a battery of angels – more harps, haloes and shiny outfits than the world will ever see in one place again. And they're all singing like it's their last chance for the big time: 'Glory to God, in the highest heaven!' they're thundering – and they can probably be heard there too. 'Peace to all God's people on earth!' Well, it's got to be something special, hasn't it – only God could throw a party like that and not get complaints from the neighbours.

Then suddenly it's all over – the sky's as black as a parson's gown, and it's as quiet as a church on a weekday. Now what? Well, there's only one thing for it.

'Let's go to Bethlehem,' they say. 'Let's see it for ourselves – this cosmic thing God's told us about.' So off they go, and what do they find? You've got it – Mary, Joseph, and the baby lying in a manger. Well, no, only the baby was in the manger – as far as we know, anyway.

Of course, what's happened to them isn't the sort of thing you keep quiet about – so, as fast as guilt follows fun, the shepherds tell them all about what they've seen and heard. Mary just listens – *really* listens – and stores it all away to think about. The shepherds? Well, they're off back to the fields, praising God and generally whooping it up over the way all the things they've heard and seen have come true.

Stories for telling

Crib sheet

Roman emperor decides to count the people – everyone goes back to their place of birth to be registered.

Joseph and Mary go to Bethlehem (despite her advanced pregnancy).

So there they are in Bethlehem – new baby in a feeding trough for a cradle – guest room not available.

> Meanwhile: shepherds in the fields. Suddenly, brighter than Blackpool.
>
> Angel – God's glory – so who wants Blackpool!
>
> Terrified.
>
> Angel: Chill out – good news.
>
> City of David – swaddling clothes – manger.

Thousands of angels – a proper party! 'Glory to God in highest heaven! Peace to all God's people!'

Suddenly, they're gone. Shepherds go to Bethlehem – find baby – tell all about it.

Mary quietly stores it all up to think about later.

Shepherds return, praising God.

The King, the Pretender and the Three Wise Guys

Based on Matthew 2:1-12

Now, you may think that being a guardian angel's a job to die for, but let me tell you it gets hairy at times – human beings can be devilish – sorry, I mean difficult – to work with.

I remember, it was about two thousand years ago: the big event of all time – God coming to earth as a human baby to share the lives of his people. We'd devoted centuries of planning, just to getting the launch right: the biggest shooting star anyone would ever have seen. And it wasn't just there for special effects. Oh, no. God had decided to make this a truly cosmic event – hence the star, see? – and he wanted visitors from a completely different culture to be there. So the star was supposed to guide them on their way, and my job was just a watching brief, really: stick around and make sure they didn't get into trouble.

So that's how I come to be watching over these three wise guys – sorry, wise men – all the way from, oh, somewhere out east, I forget the exact spot, to Bethlehem. Caspar, Melchior and Balthazar, they're called. I don't remember what they were called then, but that's what everyone calls them now. So off they set, on camels, following the star into the night sky. So far, no problem. 'So far' . . .

Now, the trouble with humans is they've always got to do things their way. You give them a half the Milky Way to guide them, and what do they do? They wonder which way to go! I ask you! So there they are, in Jerusalem, and they

Stories for telling

suddenly forget all about the star and start behaving like a committee or something.

'Where now?' asks Melchior.

'How should I know?' Balthazar answers. 'I'm an astrologer, not a clairvoyant.'

Then Caspar decides to get clever – and that's always fatal. 'We're in Jerusalem, aren't we?' he says. 'So where do you go when you're in a capital city, looking for a king?'

Balthazar's and Melchior's eyes light up like they've found the Holy Grail – except that they can't have, of course, because it doesn't exist yet. 'The palace!' they chorus.

Now that really is a seriously bad idea. The palace at Jerusalem is the home of none other than the hideously wicked, the gruesomely horrible King Herod the Great – and don't say, 'The great what?' or you'll really get me going. 'King of the Jews' is his title – but it was given to him by the Roman Emperor, not by God, so he knows he's got no right to it and spends most of his time shivering in his gold-embroidered slippers waiting for God to take it away.

So, there he is, seeing revolution round every corner, peering under the bed every night to check for terrorists, looking in the mirror every morning to check that his head's still in place – and into that scene walk none other than Caspar, Melchior and Balthazar, to say, 'Hi there, Herod – can you tell us where the *new* King of the Jews is?' Oh, yes – really calculated to make the poor guy feel better, that is!

In no time at all, Herod's got all his advisers dancing around him trying to answer his questions. You never saw such a performance. Everyone's shouting different things at him, until eventually some bright spark asks, 'What does the Bible say?' Now, Herod knows his Bible like I understand the laws of thermodynamics – he only ever reads it in the event of dire emergencies and ceremonial occasions. But they find someone who does know it, and Herod gets his answer.

The King, the Pretender and the Three Wise Guys

> 'Bethlehem – in Judea!' the scholar tells him. 'Look, it's here in the words of the prophet himself!' Then the guy gets carried away and quotes the entire prophecy including the famous 'B' word – Bethlehem! Well, that's really blown it. I mean, you know and I know that that's exactly where the three wise guys would have been if they'd stuck to following the star – but Herod didn't know it, and I'd have been a lot happier if it'd stayed that way.

All of a sudden, Herod's turning on the charm. 'Oh, how wonderful!' he spits through gritted teeth. 'Just what I've always wanted – a lovely little baby king! Look, why don't you guys go to Bethlehem, find out exactly where he is, and then come back and tell me. I'd really love to go and worship him too. And so would all my army – wouldn't they, Septimus?'

I don't hear the centurion reply – by this time, I'm flying down the corridor trying to keep up with Wossname, Thingy and Oojah-flip who're tearing back to their camels as fast as their errant little feet will carry them.

Off they go to Bethlehem, and what do they find? The star, that's what – sitting there, pointing to the place where the new King is. Everything's worked perfectly from the celestial end, but of course they had to go and do their own thing, didn't they! So, in they go and find the child, and they turn on the worshipful bit – gifts of gold, frankincense and myrrh. It would all have been terribly moving if I hadn't had wicked King Hare-brain on my mind.

> Anyway, luckily they're all worn out by now and decide to get a good night's sleep – and that gives me the chance to have a stern word with them. I decide to use the dream method – people usually take a lot more notice of dreams than they do of their own reason – and tell them in no uncertain terms not to go back to Herod. 'Go home the pretty way!' I say. 'What's the big hurry?' I say. 'Make the journey part of the holiday!'

And they do. Herod doesn't like it, but, hey, that's politics.

Stories for telling

Crib sheet

Being a guardian angel – not always easy.

About 2000 years ago – big event of all time (Incarnation).

Star – visitors from other cultures – angel monitoring progress. Comic!

Three wise guys – sorry, men – Caspar, Balthazar and Melchior.

Jerusalem: typical humans – do it their way – ignore star, ask for directions!

'What now?'

'Go to the palace'!

King Herod – pretender, really – nasty character – and paranoid.

So, three wise guys: 'Where's the *new* King of the Jews?'

In emergency, read your Bible! Herod sends for court scholars: 'In Bethlehem'.

That's blown it!

Herod: 'Do tell me where – I'd love to go and worship.'

So they find the child – gold, frankincense and myrrh.

I warn them in a dream – go home the pretty way.

Herod's not pleased – but, hey, that's politics.

Do it my way

Based on Matthew 4:1-11

Picture the scene. Jesus is just at the start of his ministry. So God publicly declares him his own special Son and sends his Holy Spirit to help him. And what does the Spirit do? Whisks him off into the desert to be tempted by the devil himself – that's what. Now, it may sound a bit strange to you, but there's method in his madness.

So, there's Jesus, in the desert – hasn't eaten for forty days, so he's probably not feeling up to much – and the devil strikes. I mean, this is his greatest challenge ever, isn't it? In the past he's only had humans to tempt, but now he's got a crack at the Son of God! Of course, normally he'd know it's futile, but this is the Son of God in human flesh and blood – so he's temptable. If the devil can crack this one, he'll really have something to tell his grand-devils when they grow up: how he scuppered God's mission by turning his own Son against him. The stakes are high. So, can he do it?

'Hey, Jesus!' he says. 'You must be desperate for food. OK, so you're the Son of God, aren't you? What's the use of a bit of power if you don't get the benefit? Just tell these stones to turn into bread – why not?'

Jesus isn't impressed. 'Well, you've got that wrong,' he says. 'My power isn't there just for my benefit. You know what the Bible says: "Bread isn't everything – we get real life by listening to what God says."'

Well, the devil's not put off – no one said that tempting

Stories for telling

God Incarnate was going to be easy. That was just the warm-up. He's got something really big up his sleeve. Next thing Jesus knows, he's standing on top of the highest pinnacle of the temple – and that's high. No rail, no safety net, just a long, long drop on to some very un-bouncy stones.

> 'Go on!' the devil whispers. 'Well, you've got to get attention, haven't you, or how are you going to make them listen? So jump off. I know my Bible, you know, and it says God won't let any harm come to you. What is it, it says? "He'll send angels to take care of you; they'll hold you in their hands and you won't even get a bruised ankle." Well, do you believe it, or what? Got faith, have you? Then prove it – jump!'

Jesus isn't falling for that – not from this height, or any other. He knows the devil's game. If Jesus' ministry can be reduced to nothing but stunts and tricks to impress the crowds, the devil really will have won. 'I've got nothing to prove!' he snaps back. 'Remember what the Bible says? "Don't tempt God!"'

Well, the devil's a bit disappointed, but he's still got the best temptation up his sleeve.

> 'Want to rule the world?' he murmurs to Jesus. 'Of course you do – that's why you've come, isn't it? Well, take a look!' And in an instant, the devil has filled Jesus' head with images of all the wonderful places in the world: all the great empires, the palaces, the harems; all the wealth of gold, silver, platinum; mountains of diamond and rubies – oh, everything you can think of, I expect. He knows that Jesus' head must be spinning with the sheer wonder of it all. 'It's all yours,' he whispers tantalisingly. 'I can give it to you. Just say you'll do things my way – team up with me – say that I'm the One. Not a lot to ask, is it – not for all this!'

The devil waits. Surely, this must be enough. I mean, who wouldn't want the world on a stick? It's only human – and Jesus *is* human. The devil can hardly contain his excitement.

'I'll tell you what,' Jesus begins.

Do it my way

'Yes?' The devil's eyes are gleaming. Here it comes! The biggest moment of a long and successful career. He begins to wonder what on earth he'll do to top this, but pushes the thought away – there'll be all eternity to think of that. Jesus is about to speak.

'What?' the devil says.

'Why don't you . . .'

The devil's really dancing around in excitement, now. 'Yes? Yes?'

'Push off!'

The devil's a bit confused. 'Push what off?'

'Yourself. Go away. Scat scram. Vamoose. Disappear. How many other ways do you need me to say it? The Bible says there's one God for us to worship and serve – and it isn't you.'

> Have you ever watched a punctured tyre slowly going down? It's a sad sight, isn't it? I almost feel sorry for the poor devil! Just as he thinks he's got the Son of God in the palm of his hand, it all slips through his fingers. He makes a sorry sight as he slinks away. But Jesus doesn't have time to feel sympathy for him, because he's got company. A company of angels have come from God to wait on him.

As for the devil – oh, don't go thinking it's all over. He'll be back.

Stories for telling

Crib sheet

Picture the scene: Jesus at the start of his ministry – declared Son of God – Holy Spirit whisks him off to the desert to be tempted.

Jesus hasn't eaten for forty days – the devil's big chance. The (now human) Son of God would be a real coup! Can he do it?

> Hungry? Use your power – turn stones into bread.

Jesus: power isn't for my benefit; bread isn't everything – we need God's word for real life.

> Pinnacle of the temple (a long drop!): jump off – Bible promises protection – prove your faith and draw the crowds!

Jesus isn't falling for that! 'I've got nothing to prove. The Bible says, "Don't tempt God."'

> All the riches of the world. 'You can have the lot – just do it my way – acknowledge my authority.'

Has it worked? The devil waits in anticipation.

(How can he top this? Think about that later.)

'Tell you what?'

'Yes?'

'Push off! Go away. Scat scram. Vamoose. Disappear. How many other ways do you need me to say it? The Bible says there's one God for us to worship and serve – and it isn't you.'

> Ever seen a tyre go down?
> Angels come to wait on Jesus.

The devil? He'll be back.

Don't panic!

Based on Mark 5:21-43

Jesus is by the seaside – seems to spend half his life there, if you ask me.

And he isn't really all that busy – until this man comes up to him in a terrible state. His daughter's dying, and he needs Jesus to save her. Now, you just don't get more desperate than that.

> He's an important man, too – Jairus, his name is, and he's a leader in the local synagogue – that's the Jewish place of worship, a bit like church is to us. And there he is, down on his knees at Jesus' feet, absolutely begging him to come and save his daughter.
>
> Well, what else would Jesus do but go with him? So he does.

So, there he is, pushing his way through the crowd – did I tell you it was crowded? Well, let's just say Trafalgar Square on New Year's Eve would look quiet compared with this. And Jesus is just starting out on his urgent mission when – wouldn't you just know it? – this woman decides she needs him too.

She's not a well woman – had a terrible illness for twelve years, she has – and the doctors have only made her feel worse, not better.

> Well, what's she supposed to do? Jesus is on his way to save someone's little girl from dying. Interrupting him right now won't exactly make this woman popular, will it?

Stories for telling

So, what do you think she does?*

She sneaks up behind Jesus and just touches the edge of his coat as he passes by.

'Well, he's got all this power,' she's thinking, 'just touching the edge will be enough.'

So she touches the hem, and what do you think happens?

Cured. Just like that! No more illness, no more pain – no problem.

Well, no problem except that Jesus has noticed – he's felt the power go out of him.

And he stops.

And he turns round to look.

And he speaks. 'Who touched my coat?'

His friends can't get over it. 'Really, Jesus! All round you, people are pushing and shoving, and you're asking who touched you?'

Jesus just keeps on looking round.

Eventually, the woman can't handle the guilt any more, so she comes forward. Now it's her turn to grovel at his feet – all fear and trembling.

And what does Jesus do?

- Does he tell her off for touching him?
- Does he call her a time-waster – say it'll be her fault if the little girl dies?
- Does he tell her he wants his bit of power back?
- What do you think he does?

---

* After all the questions of this sort, you might like to wait for an answer and adapt the next sentence accordingly – for example, 'That's right' or 'Well, I'll tell you, then.'

Don't panic!

It's amazing – he's not cross at all. 'Terrific faith!' he says. 'So, chill out, and have the healing on me.'

> Now, he's hardly got the words out when messengers arrive from Jairus' house. And they're not here to cheer him up.
>
> 'Sorry, Jairus,' they say, 'she's dead – no point in bothering the teacher now, is there?'
>
> Well, Jesus overhears, and tells Jairus, 'Don't be anxious – just trust me.'
>
> He decides to get rid of the crowd – no one follows except Peter, James and John. Together, they go on to Jairus' house.

When they get there – well, you've never heard such a racket! People are crying, wailing – and not just the family either – some people do this for a living. What a noise!

'What's all this about?' Jesus asks. 'This is one death that's not going to last very long.' Then he sends them all outside.

So there's just Jesus, with his few friends, Jairus and his wife, and the little child who's died. Then Jesus walks over to the child and takes her hand. 'Little girl,' he says, 'rise up. Come on – up!'

> And what do you think happens then? Up she gets, and starts walking about as if she's never been dead in her life – all twelve years of it!
>
> Of course, everyone's amazed.
>
> Jesus takes it in his stride, though. 'Now don't go shouting this all over the place,' he says. 'Just give her something to eat.'*

---

* The children might be puzzled about why Jesus doesn't want this story told – and they might also be too timid to ask. So why not raise the question for them and see if they have any ideas? (The most likely answer is that he doesn't want to become famous as a mere miracle worker, because the fame could get in the way of what he's really here to do.)

101

Stories for telling

Crib sheet

Jesus by the seaside – Jairus appeals for help.

Important man – begging!

Dense crowd to get through – woman decides she needs Jesus, too.

She's got a terrible illness – but afraid to interrupt important mission.

Sneaks up – touches edge of garment – sure that will do.

Instant cure.

Jesus notices (feels power leave): 'Who touched my coat?'

What a question!

Terrified woman confesses.

What does Jesus do?

Jesus reassures her – it's OK.

Messengers arrive from Jairus' house – it's too late.

Jesus takes Peter, James and John – expels mourners – death not permanent!

'Little girl, get up!'

'Tell no one – give her something to eat.'

Holy wasteful

Based on Matthew 13:1-9

Have you ever wondered about some people – whether God can really love them? I mean, *we* find it difficult, don't we? You'd think it must be impossible. And, at the very least, just going on loving someone who's never going to love you seems like a waste to me. There again, perhaps it's not a *wicked* waste.

Well, anyway, let me tell you about someone who seemed to be *really* wasteful.

> There's this farm – nothing special, just a bit of land and a few barns and things – more of a small holding, really – so you'd think the farmer would be really careful – save a lot, not take any risks, that kind of thing. Right?
>
> OK, well, he's got this bag of seeds – just the one – and it's all he's got between him and starvation. I say to him, 'You've got to be careful with that – don't waste it, now.'

Next thing I know, he's coming out of the house with his bag of seeds, and acting like a spoilt child with daddy's money – throwing it around like confetti. I mean, he's obviously completely mad – he's got this big silly grin on his face, and he's prancing around the field, laughing and singing as he goes, and scattering these seeds everywhere.

Madness – utter madness – some are landing on the path – the birds think it's their birthday, of course – and the only way he's going to get any return on *those* seeds is to make a pigeon pie.

Stories for telling

> Well, I tell you, I've known some irresponsible people in my time – give them a credit card and they make panic buying look positively respectable – but this guy, well, he's in a class of his own. I mean, who in their right mind sows wheat seeds in a rockery? Of course, it's obvious what's going to happen: I mean, it might grow a bit, but it'll soon die for lack of water – shallow soil, you see – can't retain the moisture.

Well, the seed's going everywhere – among the thistles, in the duck-pond; you name it, it lands there. And all the time I'm saying to him, 'Target your resources – make every seed count – don't go thinking thrift isn't a virtue, just because old Scrooge lost his bottle.' But it's no use; he just gives me this simpering look and coos some sentimental hogwash about love being extravagant.

> Of course, there's no justice. I mean, he only goes and ends up making a profit, doesn't he – just because some of the seed falls on good soil, and he gets a bit lucky – next thing I know he's boring us all to death in the lounge of the Hare and Hounds, bragging about this wonderful harvest he's had. Well, he says he's celebrating – bragging is my word for it.

Well, anyway, I'll have to leave it there, I've got a sermon to go and write* and I'm really struggling with it.

If anyone could give me a good, practical example of God's love and generosity it would really help me out.

Still, that's my problem. See you.

---

* Or a Sunday school session to prepare, or . . .

Holy wasteful

Crib sheet

Ever wondered about God loving 'unlovable' people? Seems a waste to love one-sidedly – but maybe not a *wicked* waste . . .

Here's a story about someone who seems really wasteful.

> Farm – small holding – need to be thrifty.
>
> He's got just one bag of seeds. Careful – don't waste it.

Crazy man – prancing around, throwing seeds everywhere.

Madness! Path – birds – need to make a pie!

Irresponsible! Sowing seeds in a rockery? No depth of soil.

Seed going everywhere! Then thistles.

> I advise: 'Target your resources – make every seed count.' Replies with sentimental hogwash about extravagant love.
>
> No justice – ends up in Hare and Hounds, bragging ('celebrating'!) about great harvest.

Got to finish – sermon to write – really struggling. Examples of God's love and generosity?

That's my problem. See you.

God's not fair – he's generous
Based on Matthew 20:1-16

Right: so there's this guy who owns a vineyard, and it's the busy season – which means he needs a bit of extra help. No problem: off he goes to the market place, which also serves as a kind of job centre. Well, seems reasonable to me – you can sell everything else from pigs to pomegranates, so why not sell your labour?

Anyway, he goes there, good and early in the morning, and does a deal – the standard daily wage for a day's work. So, they go and get cracking in the vineyard.

> Before the morning's out, he knows he's going to need more – so back to the market place he goes and finds more people hanging around there touting for work. 'You want to work?' he says. 'Go to my vineyard – I'll pay you what's fair.' Well, they probably know the guy – either that or they're desperate (which by mid-morning they might well be) – because they just take him at his word and get stuck in.

I don't know whether this guy's having an unusually good harvest or finding a lot of problems – or maybe it's just plain bad planning – but, anyway, he's back there again at lunch time and yet again at three. Each time, the same routine – promises a fair wage and sends them off to work for him.

And as if that's not enough, he goes again at five – well, we all know that the working day's virtually over at five, don't we? So there's this crew looking well fed up because they haven't done a stroke of work all day – which means they'll

God's not fair – he's generous

take no money home, and in that culture that's serious. I mean, they don't have banks, building societies and direct loan companies advertising on cable television, you know, and there's no social security, either – you don't work, you don't eat. So these guys must be panicking by now, and they probably don't ask questions like 'What's it worth?' when the landowner turns up and hires them.

> So, let's try and get a handle on this. He's got one group of labourers there who've worked a complete day – and he's promised them a day's pay. That's fair enough. Then he's got another group that only started mid-morning. So that's, what, probably three quarters of a day's pay? Then there are people who started at noon, some at three and finally this lot at five. Oh, I don't know – I'm a theologian, not a mathematician (and in theology, as we all know, it doesn't really matter if things don't add up) – so don't ask me to work it out. I just hope this guy's got a good accountant, that's all.

Well, the sun sinks slowly in the west and it's pay-off time. So he gets his foreman to line the guys up and give them their pay, starting with the ones who came last. I'm really interested to see how he's going to work this out.

But, hang on a minute, he's got it wrong. He's giving these guys who've only done an hour's work a whole day's pay. Now, I know this guy and he's – well, between you and me he's a bit soft-hearted. Obviously, he knows these men have got wives and children too, and doesn't want them to go hungry. It's very kind and all that, but it's terrible economics (even for a theologian). I mean, if he gives a day's pay for an hour's work, how much is he going to have to pay the ones who've worked all day?

> I can see they've already worked it out: they're standing there looking as if all their Passovers have come at once. Well, here come the ones who've worked for three hours. Let's see what they get? Uh-oh! I scent trouble. He's giving

Stories for telling

> them exactly the same – for three times as much work? Now, if he keeps this up, the guy's heading for an industrial relations problem on a scale I'd rather not think about. It's starting already – they're comparing wages, and the temperature's going up.

Well, he gets away with it for a bit, until the ones who started at daybreak come for their wages – and get exactly one day's standard pay. Now, the balloon goes up in no uncertain terms. 'What's this?' they're saying. 'You've given us exactly the same as those guys? We worked right through the heat of the day – sweated like Caesar in a sauna, we did – and these wimps come along for the last hour and get the same – just what do you think you're doing?'

> Me? I'd give in gracefully – a gang of angry vine-workers with cutters in their hands are not to be argued with. But I'll give this man his due – he's a cool customer. 'What's your problem?' he asks them. 'Haven't I given you what we agreed? I'd take the money and go, if I were you – or are you saying I can't spend my own money how I like? Oh, I get it – just because you're mean-spirited, you find my generosity offensive, do you?

Well, they can argue all they like, but you have to admit he's got a point. Trouble is, they're thinking about fairness – he's concerned with what people need. That's the vital difference. And that's why a lot of people who've always been stuck at the back of the queue are in for a bit of fast-track promotion – while those who think they've got fairly and squarely to the front of the queue are going to have a rude awakening.

Crib sheet

Vineyard owner – busy season – goes to market to purchase labour. Agrees a day's wage for a day's work.

Mid-morning, he needs more – back to market – 'I'll pay you what's right.'

Lunch time, he's back again (bad planning or what?) and again at three. Same routine each time.

Then back at five – workers standing there – fed up, families to keep, etc. No work means no dinner.

> Let's take stock.
> - One crew have been there all day.
> - One since mid-morning.
> - One since lunch time.
> - One since three.
> - One crew just since five.

Sundown: tells manager to pay the men off, starting with latest arrivals. How's he going to work this one out?

Gives late arrivals a day's pay – obviously knows they have same needs, but it's going to get expensive.

Gives no more to others – exactly the same for each. Mutiny!

> I'd have given in gracefully – cool customer!

'What's your problem? I kept my bargain – haven't I the right . . . mean-spirited people find generosity offensive.'

They think of fairness – he thinks of need. That's crucial difference.

That's why last will be first and first last.

Disabled access upstairs

Based on Mark 2:1-12

This is a story about faith. To be honest, I sometimes wish I had faith like this, and then I start to feel glad I haven't. I mean, it must make people very difficult to have around when they're this keen – and most of us, if we're really truthful, well, we don't like to be difficult, do we? I mean, why else would people in restaurants eat cold vegetables with smeared cutlery, and then when the nice waiter comes and says, 'Is everything all right?' just smile sweetly and say that it is? You've never done that? Well, you're braver than me – that's all I can say.

Anyway, let's get on with the story. Jesus is at home in Capernaum, when the word gets out that he's there. So in less time than it takes to say, 'Crowd-control problem', his house is jammed full of people who want to listen to him. Then the garden outside fills up and soon he's hemmed in tighter than a besieged wagon train in a western – not that he'd know what one of those is; John Wayne's well in the future.

Anyway, it's just at this time that these four guys decide to bring their friend to Jesus for healing. Why does he need four of them? Because he's paralysed, that's why – completely – can't move at all. Quadriplegic, we'd probably call him, but they're not politically correct so they say he's paralytic, which just goes to show that language doesn't travel well.

So, these four men get to the house, carrying their friend on a stretcher – well, probably a mat, to be accurate, and you can just imagine it sagging in the middle as they struggle to carry him along. These are obviously five pretty determined people. Anyway, they get to the house and they're well brassed off to find they can't get in.

> So, what do they do? Only heave the guy, still on his mat, up a flight of stairs to the roof – that's all! I don't know how you measure faith, but they must have the physical strength of about ten lumberjacks. They make it, though – huff and puff their way up the stairs and finally arrive on the top of the house.

OK, so they're there. Jesus is directly beneath them, just a matter of a few feet away. Only one problem: a nice, solid, watertight roof between them and him. And this is where I reckon the faith really comes in. I mean, they're convinced Jesus can heal this guy – right? Really convinced. And we'd probably say they're right to be convinced. But would you be convinced enough to start tearing the roof off someone's house? You're going to look a pretty special sort of a fool if you do all that and then Jesus says, 'Sorry, old thing, but it's just not what I do', aren't you? This is *so* not the way to make friends.

> Well, as I've said, this is about faith you wouldn't believe: so off comes the roof, and the mat's lowered down with the man still lying on it. To be honest, this is a bit I prefer to gloss over quickly – with my head for heights it's not good for me to dwell on ideas like this. I'll go all shivery and have to go and lie down.

Anyway, down the guy goes and lands right in front of Jesus. And Jesus is well impressed with the men's faith. So he turns to the man on the mat and says, 'You can stop feeling guilty for a start – you're completely forgiven.'

Not the thing to say in first-century Palestine when you've got law lecturers in the audience. They're off straightaway. 'Who does he think he is? God or someone? Blasphemy, that's what it is – only God can forgive sins.'

Jesus knows exactly what was going on. 'Oh, please!' he

Stories for telling

says. 'Look, the words are easy, aren't they? Anyone can *claim* to forgive sins – it's completely unverifiable. But what if I say, "Pick up your bed and walk"? Now, that would show a bit of authority wouldn't it! I mean it either works or it doesn't. So let's try, shall we – then we'll see if I've got any authority or not. OK, young feller-me-lad – on your feet, pack up your mat and tread that homeward road!'

Of course, they're all watching. I mean, here's the test, isn't it? If Jesus is just a pretentious nobody, then the man will just lie there looking pathetic. But what's this? Suddenly, he's on his feet, slinging his mat over his shoulder and picking his way through the crowds with the kind of delicate footwork that could dazzle Muhammad Ali in his heyday!

That showed them. What the scribes said at that moment, history doesn't relate – probably because it was either nothing at all or unprintable. As for the rest of the crowd, though, they were flabbergasted – praising God, and saying that they'd never seen anything like it in their lives. Which, of course, they hadn't.

Crib sheet

Story about faith – mixed feelings about it. Most of us like the quiet life, don't like to be thought difficult – hence not complaining in restaurants.

Jesus at home in Capernaum – crowds in and around the house.

> Four guys bring their paralysed friend to Jesus on a stretcher – well, mat, actually. Can't get into the house.
>
> Up stairs, on to roof – quite a feat! What now?

Jesus just beneath them – roof in way. Now, they must really believe to start tearing roof off!

Man lowered down, right in front of Jesus.

Jesus: 'No more guilt!'

Scribes object – Jesus hasn't the authority to forgive sins.

> Jesus argues: Anyone can say the words – do they work is the question. Forgiveness is unverifiable – that's why 'Get up and walk' is the real test.
>
> So, he says it. People watch in anticipation.

Man gets up, picks up bed and does some nifty footwork to get through the crowd.

Everyone's flabbergasted – never seen anything like it in their lives.

Who's in and who's out?

Based on Mark 7:24-30

'Charity begins at home,' people say – and that's right, but it doesn't mean it has to end there too. Same with mission. We've got to start somewhere, and where we are is probably best. But how do we know when it's time to broaden the vision? Don't know – maybe there's not a single answer to that – but one way is to listen to people, even if they're not the people we expect to hear it from. And that's what Jesus does in this story.

> It all starts when Jesus is taking a break. Well, you now how it is. It's Murphy's law, isn't it: just as you decide that you're exhausted and need a holiday – right at the time when you need a bigger case load like Job needs extra boils – just at that precise moment, something comes up. So, there's Jesus, off on a retreat with his disciples, somewhere a good way away from his usual haunts – in the Tyre region, in fact. And it looks like he's managed to get away without being recognised. Then, just as he goes in through the door of the house where he's staying, he hears a voice.

Yes, you've guessed it – he's been recognised. It's someone wanting help. There'll always be people wanting help, and you have to draw a line somewhere. And this woman's definitely over the line: she's a Syro-Phoenician woman – mixed race, and neither of them Jewish. Well, right now, Jesus' mission's just beginning and he's focusing it for best effect. So, all ways round, he doesn't need a distraction. You can understand the woman, though: her daughter's in a terrible state – seems to be possessed or something – and

Who's in and who's out?

Mum's desperate, so she comes and kneels down at Jesus' feet, absolutely begging him to exorcise the demon and heal her daughter.

Now, like I said, you've got to draw the line or everything just gets chaotic. So Jesus looks at her and says, 'Look, I'm really sorry, but I'm still in phase one, right now. I mean, I'm still feeding the family, and that means children first – dogs can be fed later.'

> I know that sounds pretty shocking to you and me – but in their context it's just a family image that's about prioritising things. No decent parent's going to feed the family pets when the children are starving. And right now the children of Israel are starving!

You might think she'd be put off and just go away to wait her turn. But this woman's shrewd: she's got a quick mind and a rapid-fire tongue – isn't afraid of telling it how it is, you know? So straightaway, she's back with an answer.

> 'OK, fair enough – but even while you're feeding the children, the dogs get the scraps that fall on the floor, don't they? I mean, they don't wait right until the end of the meal, do they? So, fine, I'll just be a dog and take whatever's left.'

Jesus just looks at her for a moment. Everyone's wondering what he's going to do – I mean, no one who wanted something from him has dared to argue with him like that before. How's he going to react?

> 'Well!' he says. 'For saying that, you can just go home – and you'll find your daughter well. Congratulations!'

So, she does – goes back home, finds her daughter lying on the bed as calm and unruffled as the Serpentine in summer. I wonder whether she knows that this is a moment in history: the mission of Christ has begun at home – like charity. But it isn't going to end there.

Stories for telling

Crib sheet

'Charity begins at home' – but it doesn't end there. Mission, likewise.

So, when's it time to widen it? Listen to the outsiders – as Jesus does here.

> Jesus taking a break – needs a holiday – just the time when he'll be wanted!
>
> Arriving at house in Tyre – accosted by a Syro-Phoenician woman. Daughter's ill – needs an exorcism. Begs Jesus to help.

This is where the line is: this is phase one – still feeding the family. Children first, then dogs.

Sounds horrible – in context, just a family image – children are still starving!

> Shrewd woman – not easily put off.
>
> 'Fine – but don't the dogs get the scraps, even while the meal's in progress?'

Wow! Fancy arguing with Jesus! What'll he do, now?

'For saying that, you can . . . go home – daughter well.'

Does she know what an historic moment this is? Jesus' mission – like charity – begins at home.

But it won't end there.

Who does he think he is?

Based on Luke 4:14-30

I tell you, I don't want to witness anything like this again – except from a very safe distance. In all my days as a keeper of the faith, I've never seen such a thing happen in a synagogue – and it's not a nice thing to be caught up in the middle of, I can tell you.

It all starts with Jesus – well, you might have known, mightn't you! I mean, the guy's hardly been baptised five minutes, and he's been out in the desert ever since, communing with God or some such nonsense. Anyway, he comes back, all full of enthusiasm – full of the Spirit, as his kind might say – and goes round the synagogues preaching. Then, the dreaded day arrives: he walks into mine.

Well, I know it probably isn't wise, but I can't just ignore the guy – he's getting to be something of a local personality. If I don't give him something to do, it'll look like sour grapes. So – purely out of politeness, mind you – I give him a reading to do. Isaiah – not the best choice, now I look back, but there you are.

Anyway, he stands up to read, and so far it's just like any ordinary Sabbath. No one's really paying that much attention, to be honest, which isn't an entirely bad thing – I'm quite happy with a certain level of apathy, it keeps things nice and predictable.

It's Isaiah, this particular morning. You probably know the passage – and as soon as he starts to read it, I know I've made a mistake.

Stories for telling

'The Spirit of God is upon me,' he reads, 'because he's anointed me to proclaim good news to the poor. He's sent me to announce freedom to captives, sight to blind people, liberation for the oppressed. In short, to proclaim God's year of jubilee.'

Well, that's the apathy gone out of the window. Suddenly, the air's tingling with anticipation – and I don't like it. He hands the scroll back to the official and sits down, and there's not an eye in the place looking anywhere but at him. Something about the way he read it: almost as if he had some kind of authority – which, of course, he hasn't.

> Then he speaks. 'Right now,' he says, 'right now, in this very place, this scripture's been fulfilled – even as you listened to it.'
>
> Well, it's a load of nonsense, of course, but you try and tell that to the congregation! I mean, you'd think they'd been waiting all their lives just to meet this character – and no one's paying any attention to me!

'Ooh, listen!' one of them says. 'Don't he speak good?' I must make a note to re-launch my course on Language and Grammar in the Synagogue.

Then they're all saying, 'Not bad for a carpenter's son, eh?' And that seems to be a pivot, because they seem to sense that someone like him has no right to be eloquent – and things start to swing back my way again.

'Just a carpenter's son!' someone says. I'm just about to capitalise on it when Jesus goes and throws in a real firecracker.

> 'Oh, right!' he says. 'I suppose you're going to quote that old proverb to me: "Doctor, heal yourself – why can't you do miracles in your own town like we've been hearing you've done in Capernaum?" Well, I'm telling you straight, the only place a prophet doesn't get the respect he needs is in his home town.'

Who does he think he is?

Well, by now, I'm feeling a lot better. To begin with, he's rapidly throwing away his popularity – which can only be good for me – and, to be honest, he's telling them some home truths I've often wanted to throw their way. So I just let him get on with it. And, boy, does he get on with it.

'The reality is,' he says to them, 'that there were plenty of widows in Israel during Elijah's great famine, but where was he sent? All the way to Zarephath, in Sidon – that's where.'

Oh, this was wonderful stuff! This lot had never appreciated my ministry, and I'd have loved to say this to them but, of course, you can't when you're a professional – too much to lose. This guy's doing it for me, and digging his own grave at the same time. I couldn't have planned it better if I'd planned it at all! And still he's going on at them.

> 'And what about Elisha?' he's roaring above the din. 'Do you reckon there weren't people in Israel with skin diseases for him to heal? But it had to be Naaman – a Syrian soldier – who came to him for healing, didn't it!'

Well, that does it! Suddenly they're on him like a pack of hyenas – I'd often wondered what they reminded me of – screaming for blood and threatening to spill it all over my newly sanded parquet floor. So I'm screaming over the noise: 'Outside – get him outside!' And that's when it gets a bit out of hand. Outside isn't far enough – through the town they drag him, right to the top of the hill and up to the cliff top. Oh, my holy prayer shawl – they're going to throw him over the top. Now, this is getting well scary – beyond anything I'd been expecting. And that's when he does it.

> I'm on the edge of the crowd, so the first thing I know is when it all starts going quiet. What's this mean – have they done it? Have they topped the guy? Then the crowd begins to part, and there he is, striding through the middle of them away from the cliff edge. They're just falling back and letting him through. And as he gets close to me, I can

Stories for telling

> see why. That look – that expression on his face: I don't know how to describe it – a mixture of deadly determination and complete serenity. What's the word I'm after? Yes, that's it: authority. He walks toward me, and for some reason I can't move – just rooted to the spot, I am. By the time I've got myself together, I'm looking at his back disappearing into the town.

Well, I've never been the same since – *nothing's* ever been the same since! I tell you, if I knew what it is that guy's got, I'd bottle it and use it for bath oil.

Crib sheet

I don't want to witness anything like this again!

Jesus – only baptised five minutes – enthusiasm! Getting famous – then walks into my synagogue . . .

Don't be churlish – ask him to read. No one's really bothering – no bad thing.

> Isaiah: Spirit of God – good news to the poor – freedom to captives – sight to blind – free the oppressed – God's jubilee year.

Air tingling – sits down – every eye riveted on him. 'This is the time.' Everyone's amazed – then it turns to scepticism – just a carpenter's son!

'Doctor, heal yourself – do miracles here too! Prophet not without honour . . .'

> This is OK! Home truths – and cooking his own goose at the same time!

'Widows in Israel but Elijah sent to Zarephath, Sidon.'

> Wonderful! I can't get away with this – too much to lose – and he's digging his own grave too!

'Naaman – Syrian healed by Elisha – no lepers in Israel?'

That's it – mob attacks – drags Jesus out, through town, up hill, to cliff edge.

> I'm on edge of crowd – hear it go quiet – see crowd parting.
>
> Jesus strides through – that face! Determination and serenity.

Authority! Walks past me – can't respond.

Never the same since. If I knew what he's got I'd bottle and bath in it!

I know I'm forgiven

Based on Luke 7:36-50

This is a story about something really embarrassing that happened to Jesus. Well, let me put it another way: other people seemed to find it embarrassing – positively cringe-making, in fact – and so would I, if I'd been there, but Jesus just didn't seem bothered at all.

OK, let me set the scene: he's been invited to dinner – by a Pharisee of all people. Most of the Pharisees hate Jesus, so he's likely to be prepared for anything, anyway. The guy probably just wants Jesus there so he can find some way of showing him up – not to be friends with him. Well, if that's how it is, then this woman gives the Pharisee exactly what he wants.

They're all sitting there around the table – well, not so much sitting as reclining, sort of half-lying, on couches, propped up on one elbow. Yes, I know – it sounds odd to me too – and uncomfortable – but that's what they used to do. Anyway, everything seems to be going nice and smoothly when this woman just comes bursting in off the street – which is where she usually does her business, if you get my drift. I mean, she is *so* not the kind of person a Pharisee wants in his house.

Now, she's not come empty-handed: she's got a present for Jesus – a jar made of alabaster (think of Ming dynasty porcelain and you've probably got the value of it in modern terms about right). This is real high-value stuff – not the kind of jar you keep your everyday bath-oil in – so the perfume in it's probably something pretty spectacular too. And what does she do? She goes round behind Jesus so she can get to his

I know I'm forgiven

feet as he lies there, and bursts into tears. I tell you, this is embarrassing – and at the meal table too. Jesus' feet are running wet with this woman's tears, and they're going to have to interrupt the meal and send a servant for a towel.

No, I'm wrong – she's thought of that too. Oh, this is gross: she's only using her own hair as a towel to dry Jesus' feet – I mean, no one knows how often she washes it, or what might be living in there. Then, when she's finished – well, she's not finished at all – then she starts kissing his feet, all over, and pouring this perfume over them. I mean, this is so not the way to behave!

> On the other hand, this couldn't be better from the Pharisee's point of view. 'Got him now!' he's thinking. 'So, Jesus is supposed to be some sort of prophet or holy man, is he? Well, in that case, he should know just what sort of woman he's got mauling him – sinner doesn't begin to describe her.'

You know, it's almost as if Jesus knows what the guy's thinking. 'Simon,' he says, 'I've got something to say to you.'

Well, Simon probably thinks he's about to get a public apology or something. 'Oh, speak, teacher,' he says. 'Please, speak!'

So Jesus does. 'Look, there's this money-lender, see, and he's lent money to a couple of guys who can't pay. One of them owes him five hundred pounds, and the other – well, let's say about fifty. You with me so far? Good – because here comes the complicated bit. The lender just writes off the debts – completely – no strings attached. Still with me? Good – hang in there, Simon, because you're going to learn something. Now, here's the question: which of those guys is going to love the money-lender most?'

> You can tell that Simon's almost disappointed. I mean, he's not going to show off his brain-power with this, is he? It's easy! 'The one who had the biggest debt written off,' he answers.

Stories for telling

'Got it in one!' Jesus says. 'Nice bit of judgement there, old lad. Now, take this case, then. See this woman? I came into your house and I might as well not have been here. No water to wash my feet after the walk – I mean, even common courtesy demands that, let alone the law that you lot are always so proud of keeping to the letter – but she's washed my feet with her very own tears, and used her own hair for a towel to dry them. TLC doesn't get much more personal than that, does it! Now, you know that a welcome kiss is traditional in these parts – I mean, it's the done thing – but did I get one? Not on your sweet prayer-shawl, I didn't. She's kissed me, though – all over my feet. Oh, yes – and what about anointing my head – another of these little rituals that you Pharisees claim never to forget. I mean, tell me I'm old fashioned, but I distinctly missed that when I arrived – had to wait for this woman to come in and anoint my feet with wonderful perfume. OK, Mr Law-keeper – you tell me who's the sinner round here. You see, *her* sins – and I know there are plenty of them – they've been forgiven, and that's why she's got all this love just bursting to come out of her. Now, someone whose experience of forgiveness is limited – well, they're not going to have much love to give, are they? Mentioning no names, of course.'

By now, Simon's gobsmacked – lying there on his couch, opening and closing his mouth like a goldfish in a trance – but with absolutely nothing to say. That doesn't matter, though, because Jesus hasn't finished yet. He turns to the woman and says, 'Your sins are forgiven.'

Now, he's done it – everyone knows only God can forgive sins, so he's in big trouble now. 'Who does this guy think he is?' they're all asking. 'What sort of human being forgives sins?'

Jesus doesn't even dignify that with an answer. He just keeps talking to the woman. 'Off you go, then,' he says. 'No worries, no hassles, no more guilt and all that stuff – your faith's saved you.'

Now, I guess we all know people like that Pharisee – and

I know I'm forgiven

they seem like pretty regular sort of folk. I mean, far be it from me to be judgemental about petty-minded hypocrisy . . .

But I know whom I'd rather have around when I'm needing a bit of love.

Stories for telling

Crib sheet

Story about something really embarrassing – but Jesus not bothered.

Jesus invited to dinner by Pharisee – probably to try and show him up.

All sitting – well, reclining, actually – at table when this woman bursts in – not desirable!

Brings alabaster jar of perfume – weeps over Jesus' feet, dries with her hair (gross!), kisses feet and applies perfume. What a way to behave!

Pharisee: If he were a prophet, he'd know . . .

Jesus: 'Simon, I've got something to say to you.'

Pharisee (probably expecting apology): 'Please do!'

Jesus: Money-lender – two debtors, one owing £500, the other £50. Forgives them both – who'll love him more?

Simon: 'Easy – the first one.'

Jesus: Not welcomed properly according to law and tradition:
- No foot-washing (but she's used her own tears and hair).
- No kiss – she's kissed feet continually.
- No anointing: she's anointed feet.

Many sins forgiven = loves much.
Someone forgiven little = loves little.

Woman is forgiven – scandal! – 'Go in peace.'

I know whom I'd rather have around when I need some love!

What do you mean, 'Neighbour'?

Based on Luke 10:25-37

Anyone got a good neighbour or really caring friend? Want to tell us about them?*

Anybody ever had a nice surprise when someone we didn't expect to be kind helped us?†

Trouble is, how do you define 'neighbour'? And that's the question facing Jesus in our story.

> It all starts with some smart-alec lawyer asking about the law – and the whole of the Jewish law, as we know, comes down to two things: love God, and love your neighbour. But that's not complicated enough for this guy, so he goes and asks another question: 'Who counts as my neighbour?' Well, to a storyteller like Jesus, that's as good as dropping a hat. And this is the story he tells:

There's a man who decides to walk from Jerusalem to Jericho. Yes, I know it's not a good idea, going down that road on your own, but he does – and, as we'll see, he's not the only one. Anyway, he's not gone far before he's spotted by some muggers – and when I say 'spotted', I mean black and blue. Beaten to a pulp he is, before they make off with his cash, clothes and most of his dignity.

So there he is, lying on the road in the burning sun, with his head in a spin and one foot in the grave, when suddenly he hears footsteps. It's a priest, walking along the same road.

---

* Listen to the answers and respond as appropriate.
† Likewise.

Stories for telling

Well, it's got to be good news, hasn't it? I mean, you wouldn't expect a priest to ignore a guy in this kind of trouble, would you?

> Probably not – but you'd be wrong. He doesn't just pass by without stopping – he even crosses the road to do it. Well, it's nasty stuff, blood, isn't it – don't want to get that on your nice priestly robes, do you!

So, the guy just carries on lying there – not a lot of choice in the matter, really – until the next footsteps are heard. Just as long as it isn't another priest, that's all . . . It isn't a priest. Well, that's a relief! No, it's a Levite – a different kind of religious minister – and he's walking right by, just the same as the priest did – but not before he's crossed over the road to maintain a safe distance. I mean, it's enough to make you lose your faith in religion, isn't it? Not God, mind you – just religion.

> Anyway, all the time he lies there, the sun's getting hotter and hotter, and his mouth's getting dryer and dryer. He's not alone, though – I mean you're never alone when you're lying outside in the heat, covered in blood. He's got plenty of company: flies, gnats, probably a curious spider or two, and doubtless by now a really attentive flock of vultures, circling overhead and waiting. Just waiting . . .

More footsteps on the road. Someone else coming. What's this? Oh, great – that's all he needs. This guy's not a priest – or a Levite – this one's a Samaritan. Terrific. A Samaritan's more likely to kick a Jew who's down than try and help him – which is also what the Jew would do to the Samaritan if the sandal were on the other foot. So our poor, petrified friend is just bracing himself for the impact when the Samaritan starts giving him first aid.

Unbelievable! I mean, he's only treating him like one of his own race, that's all! He's wiping the wounds clean, adding some oil to help them heal, and what's this? Wine? I mean,

What do you mean, 'Neighbour'?

is nothing too much for this guy? Well, it probably makes a good, if rather expensive, antiseptic. Anyway, he does all this, puts on nice clean dressings, and then picks the man up and puts him on his own mule. And all the time, he's saying nice, reassuring things about 'seeing he's all right' and 'getting him cared for'.

> So, they're off down the road, the Samaritan walking so that the Jew can have the mule, and they come to a hotel. Next thing the casualty knows is that he's in a nice, clean bed, with en-suite water-jug and washing bowl, and the Samaritan – you know, this hated enemy that he wouldn't trust to give him the time of day – is handing over money to the innkeeper and saying, 'Just take care of him until next time I'm here, and I'll pay you any extra then.'

OK, so Jesus has told this story, and he turns to the lawyer and asks, 'Which of those three characters was a neighbour to the man who got mugged?'

Well, the lawyer can only give one answer, can't he? 'The one who helped him,' he says – probably through gritted teeth, but scripture doesn't relate.

So Jesus says, 'Fine – now, why don't you go and act like him?'

Stories for telling

Crib sheet

Anyone got a good neighbour – caring friend? Want to tell us?
(Listen and respond appropriately.)
Ever been nicely surprised by a 'bad' person?
(Likewise.)
Problem: definitions – that's the challenge for Jesus in this story.

> Smart-alec lawyer: 'Love God and neighbour – fine – but who *is* my neighbour?' Hat drops: storytelling time!

Guy walks from Jerusalem to Jericho (alone!) – spotted by muggers.

Lying on road in sun – head in a spin, one foot in the grave – priest comes along. Surely, won't ignore?

Not only walks by – crosses road! Blood – not nice!

Next one along: Levite – does same. Enough to make you lose your faith in religion.

> So, victim left lying there . . . Not alone, though: flies, gnats, spiders, probably vultures . . .
> More footsteps: Samaritan. Oh, great – probably kick him while he's down!

Unbelievable – treats him well! Dressings, oil, wine – free donkey ride!

Takes him to hotel – pays in advance – 'If it comes to more, I'll settle later.'

> OK, so Jesus has told the story – turns to lawyer: 'Who was the neighbour?'

Lawyer: 'The one who helped.'
'Then why not be like that, too?'

A fool and his money

Based on Luke 12:13-21

It all begins – as so often – with someone in the crowd around Jesus asking a question. Read the Gospels, and we find there was more often than not a crowd in the vicinity, and, generally speaking, they had even less of a clue about Jesus than the disciples did – which at times is really saying something.

> So, there's someone in the crowd who obviously thinks Jesus is there as his personal advocate, to make everything right for him. 'Hey, Jesus!' he says 'Tell my brother he's got to divide up the family inheritance with me.'
>
> Now, just in case we're tempted to think this is a matter of common justice, and we'd expect Jesus to be on the side of the injured party – well, let's just say it probably wasn't as simple as it seemed. Family disputes about property seldom are, even now – and in that culture there were some really interesting complications.

Anyway, I'm not getting into that now. The point is that Jesus isn't getting drawn in. 'Look, mate,' he says, 'who made me your lawyer?' Before the guy can recover from that, he turns to the rest of the crowd. 'Watch yourselves!' he says. 'Don't get dragged down by greed – because there's a lot more to the meaning of your life than how much dosh you've got.' Then he goes on to tell them this story.

> There's this guy, OK – landowner – and his land does really well and gives him a harvest to die for (hang on to that thought – it's going to be relevant). So he starts thinking,

Stories for telling

> 'What on earth am I going to do with it all? I mean, we're talking mega-shekels here, if I handle it properly. I know: I'll get the builders in – they can start by knocking down these fiddly little barns and build some real ones – big enough for everything I've got. Then I can hoard it all away – because it's mine – because I grew it – so I can do what I like with it, can't I? Then I'll have enough to keep body and soul together for ever – no more worries, no more work – just years of wonderful self-indulgence. I can't wait to get started on that.'

Now, I think the guy's missing a thing or two here. I mean, for a start, he didn't make all that stuff grow, did he? It's the produce of the land – and under Hebrew law no one can truly own land – the best we can do is borrow it from God. Well, he's forgotten that for a start. And what's all that about keeping body and soul together? He's in for a shock there too – because it's not money that does that. And he's about to find that out – big time.

> This is where God takes a hand in things. 'OK, sunshine!' he says. 'You really think you've got this kind of power? "Keep body and soul together", indeed! I never heard such rubbish in all my eternity. Tell you what: you can keep the body, but I'll have the soul. That should get your fancy ideas back in perspective – pity you won't be around to benefit from it, but that's the way the harvest winnows out, isn't it! So, who's going to benefit from all that stuff now? Because it certainly won't be you.'

So, that's it – by the morning, he's dead. I mean, body has *so* been separated from soul. And all that's left to show for a lifetime of hard, backbreaking work is a mountain of rotting grain. Well, I suppose the local wildlife will benefit, but I can't help thinking there must be more to a meaningful life than that.

A fool and his money

Crib sheet

Begins with someone in the crowd asking a question – thinks Jesus is his personal advocate!

'Tell my brother to divide the family inheritance with me.'

More complicated than it sounds – let's leave it at that.

> Jesus warns against greed – more to the meaning of life than dosh.
>
> Tells story: landowner – land produces a crop to die for (hold on to that image). What's he going to do?

'I'll pull down these fiddly barns and build big ones – hoard my crops – no more worries – live in luxury – keep body and soul together.'

> Isn't he missing something? *His* crops? Can't really 'own' land. 'Keep body and soul together'? Money can't do that.
>
> God takes a hand: 'You've got big ideas! You keep the body – I'll have the soul. Now who's going to benefit?'

Morning: he's dead – body and soul separated!

All that's left to show for his life: rotting crops. Food for wildlife, I suppose – but there must be more to life than that!

Jesus confronts Jerusalem

Based on Luke 19:28-48

This is the moment the disciples have been waiting for: Jesus is going to Jerusalem. At last, they think, he's going to declare himself king – the big takeover the whole nation's been expecting for centuries. We can feel the excitement mounting as they get to the Mount of Olives: Jerusalem is in sight! Jesus stops – somewhere around Bethphage and Bethany – and sends two of the disciples on a mission. 'Go into the village,' he says. 'There's a colt tied up there – one that no one's ever ridden before. I want you to bring it to me. And if anyone asks, "Why are you untying that colt?" just say, 'The Lord needs it", and that'll be OK. OK?'

> So the disciples go into the village, and there it is – just the way he said it would be. As they start to untie it, they hear an angry voice. 'Hey! You two! What're you doing untying that colt?' It's the owners of the colt – and they don't look as if they're asking just out of curiosity.
>
> All it takes is those four words: 'The Lord needs it.'
>
> Soon as they hear that, they change completely. 'Oh, my dear fellows, why didn't you say so before? Enough said – help yourselves.'

So they bring the animal to where Jesus is waiting, but they're not really happy with it – it's not even got a saddle. So they improvise – throw their coats over it – and help Jesus on to its back.

I tell you, it's a strange sight as they approach the city:

Jesus, just in the clothes he always wears, sitting on this funny little colt – a sort of apology for a horse – and the people around him spreading their cloaks on the road for him to ride over. It's actually kind of impressive, really, isn't it – doing their best to give him the red-carpet treatment, even though they haven't got so much as a wine-stained hearth-rug between them.

> So, now he's on the path down the mountainside, and everyone's going ape – praising God, shouting about all the things they remember seeing Jesus do. And as they get nearer the capital, they really get going: 'Congratulations!' they're shouting. 'Congratulations to the new king – the one who comes in God's name!' Then another lot start up with 'Peace on earth and glory in heaven!' and before anyone can say, 'Politically inexpedient' the whole thing's turned into a victory parade.

Now, among them are some people you might wish weren't there. You've got it – some Pharisees are in the crowd around Jesus. And they don't like the way this is turning out one little bit. 'Hey, Teacher,' they're saying, 'can you shut this lot up? Go on – just tell them to button it, OK?'

Jesus just shrugs his shoulders. 'No point,' he says. 'I mean, if they did shut up, the stones themselves would probably start yelling – it's just that kind of day.'

Then the mood changes. They're getting near Jerusalem now, and all Jews really love Jerusalem, so why's Jesus in tears all of a sudden – and on a day like this too? 'If you only knew!' he's saying. 'If you only knew what it really means to call yourself "Peace"!' Oh, by the way, did you know that the 'Salem' part of Jerusalem means 'Peace'? Well, there you are. No one really knows what the first half means. It could be 'Possession' or perhaps 'Foundation' – so maybe the city's founded on peace, or in some way to be in Jerusalem is to possess peace? I don't know – I have enough trouble with English, and anyway I'm wandering off the point.

Stories for telling

> So, there's Jesus, crying like a baby over his beloved Jerusalem. 'All that is hidden from you,' he says, 'and, boy, are you going to pay the price for that! First'll come the siege, but that won't last long – the enemy will be right inside, crushing you and destroying you – even the unborn children – and by the time they've finished there won't be one stone left on top of another. And why? Because when God himself visited you with an offer you shouldn't refuse, you hadn't got the vision to recognise the moment!'

This is heart-rending stuff, isn't it? I don't hear any malice in Jesus' voice – just a terrible, terrible grief for a city and people he loves to bits. The tears are still shining in his eyes when he gets to the temple, but the sorrow very quickly turns to anger and boils over. The place is full of traders, selling stuff – right there in the courts of the holy temple itself. Not for long, though – not when Jesus gets in among them – suddenly they're all scurrying for the exits, grabbing what they can as they go – money rolling about the floor and people getting their fingers trodden on as they go grubbing around in the dirt trying to pick it up. And all the time, Jesus is yelling at them. 'You know what scripture calls this place?' he roars. 'A house of prayer, that's what! And just look what you've made of it – as vile a thieves' kitchen as you'll find anywhere! I bet you're really proud of yourselves!'

> But, you know, it's the strangest thing: no one lifts a finger against him. I bet if you or I tried that in Leicester Cathedral* we'd be banged up before we got to the second sentence! But Jesus calmly goes back to the temple every day to teach, and no one lays a finger on him. Oh, they want to – no mistake about that. I mean, he's done what no one's ever achieved before: he's got the priests, scribes and elders to agree about something – which is that they want him dead.

---

* or wherever's local to you . . .

Trouble is, they can't touch him – not without causing an even bigger riot – because the people are absolutely lapping it up. So they'll just have to wait: they know their time will come.

Stories for telling

Crib sheet

This is the moment disciples have been waiting for: Jesus is gong to Jerusalem – takeover bid? Mount of Olives – sends disciples for colt.

'The Lord needs it.'

Coats placed on colt's back – Jesus set upon it.

Cloaks on road – red-carpet treatment.

> During descent, chant starts: 'Peace on earth . . . Glory in heaven . . . Congratulations to the king . . .'
>
> Pharisees: 'Shut them up.'
>
> Jesus: 'No point – stones would shout!'

Change of mood – Jesus in tears for Jerusalem – 'If only you knew what "peace" meant.'

(That's what 'Salem' means . . . but wandering off point!)

'It's all hidden' – predicts siege, destruction – 'didn't recognise time of God's visitation.'

> Then anger in temple: traders thrown out.
>
> Odd – couldn't do that in (for example) Leicester Cathedral.

Jesus has achieved impossible: united priests, scribes and elders!

They can't touch him, though – people love him – have to wait their moment.

A passion for people

Based on Luke 23:1-49

This is a love story. Oh, don't worry, it's not a man-woman thing – I leave that stuff to tabloids and television. This is a different kind of love. And you'd better have your tissues ready because it's a sad one. Oh, there'll be a happy ending, but not today. I'm going to leave that for later, because I reckon there's a lot of really powerful stuff about hope here – and we might miss it if we just go leaping into the happy ending. So, are you ready?

> Jesus has been arrested. They've finally got him. Real heroic stuff, it was: they sneaked up on him, mob-handed, in a deserted place at night. Oh, yes: you don't see courage like that every day – thank goodness! Anyway, they've given him a good grilling at the High Priest's house, and now he's being dragged over to the Roman Governor's place. Now, don't misunderstand me: officially, the priests don't have any time for the Romans, and don't recognise the authority of the Governor – but this is an emergency, and needs must when the devil drives . . .

So, there they are, in the Governor's headquarters, and they're really scraping the barrel to pin something on him. 'We heard him leading people astray,' they're saying. 'He told people not to pay their taxes, and he reckons he's the Messiah – that's "king", to you, or near enough, anyway.'

Now, that's really inventive stuff, that is. Jesus never told people not to pay taxes – quite the reverse, in fact – but they're desperate, which is when most of us get tempted to be a bit liberal with the truth. And as for this 'Messiah'

Stories for telling

stuff, well, if he ever did say that, he didn't mean it the way they're making it sound – and they know it. And the sad thing is these are good people – respected religious leaders. I mean, if fear can make *them* do this, what hope for the rest of us?

> Sorry, I'm getting carried away again. So, back to Pilate. He looks at Jesus – who by now is looking pretty pathetic, it has to be said: tied up, bruised, probably shattered after a sleepless night on his feet. 'You?' he says incredulously. 'Are *you* a king?'
>
> Jesus just answers, 'You're the one who's saying that.'

So Pilate turns to the priests and the rest. 'Oh, come on, you guys – you cannot be serious! You're not telling me this character's some sort of threat to Rome, surely!'

'You should hear him,' they answer. 'He's got the whole of Galilee up in arms.'

Now, that sounds calculated to frighten Pilate, but he's obviously got their number. 'Oh, he's Galilean, then?' he asks. 'Well, in that case, it's King Herod's problem – go and give him some grief, instead of me.'

> Herod's well glad – been wanting to meet Jesus for years – hoping to see some amazing stunt or other, no doubt. Jesus isn't rising to the bait, though, and keeps shtum – whatever Herod asks him. So Herod and his soldiers have a bit of fun – dress him like a king and take the time out to ridicule him – and finally send him back to Pilate wearing a posh robe.

So Pilate has another go at the priests and elders. 'Look,' he says, 'you brought this guy to me with all kinds of stuff about being a dangerous revolutionary. Well, I can't find any problem with him, and neither can Herod. As far as I can see, the man's harmless enough – so I'll give him a flogging, but that's it – he goes free after that.

A passion for people

Now, don't get your hopes up – it isn't over yet. The rabble start yelling and screaming that they want Jesus executed, and if anyone's gong to be released it'd better be Barabbas. Now, he really *is* a nasty piece of work – put in prison for rebellion and murder – and they want *him*? Anyway, Pilate gives it another try, but they aren't having any of it, so eventually the guy gives in to the mob – like the great politician he reckons he is – lets Barabbas go and sends Jesus to be crucified.

One of the passers-by, Simon, from Cyrene, gets press-ganged into carrying Jesus' cross – and all kinds of other people follow too, some of them women who are well upset – and showing it. Jesus turns to them and says, 'It's not me you should be crying for. Spare some tears for yourselves and your children. The time's going to come when people who haven't got children to worry about will be the lucky ones.'

Well, they eventually get to the site of execution: the 'Place of the Skull'. Jesus is crucified, along with a couple of rebels, one each side of him. It's the most incredible moment: as they're doing it, Jesus is praying for them. No kidding! 'Forgive them, Father,' he says. 'They just haven't a clue what it is they're doing.' Well, you've got to hand it to the guy – I reckon most of us would have some very different things to say. And while he's dying, what are the people around doing? Gambling for his clothes and shouting insults at him – that's what. And over the top of him, as he hangs there, naked, blood-stained and completely pitiful, they put a big sign, full of malicious irony: 'This is Jesus of Nazareth, King of the Jews!'

There's something about him, though – even now – and it seems to get through to one of the rebels. The other one's mocking Jesus, with everybody else, when this guy rounds on him and puts him in his place. 'You really are a lost cause, aren't you!' he says. 'I mean, we're guilty, we are – getting what we deserve – but this guy's never done a wrong thing in his life.' Then he turns to Jesus and says,

Stories for telling

'Remember me, won't you – when you come into your kingdom?'

'I'm telling you straight,' Jesus answers, 'this very day you're gong to be in Paradise with me.' Powerful stuff – just to think of a conversation like that going on between two tortured men! Anyway, by now it's noon and as dark as night. Three hours, the darkness stays – three long, inexplicable hours. And then a really awesome thing happens: there's this dreadful rending sound, and the curtain of the temple – the barrier between the ordinary people and the holy of holies – is just ripped into shreds from top to bottom. Then, before anyone can wonder what's gong on, Jesus gives this huge shout. 'Father!' he calls. 'I'm committing my spirit into your keeping!' And those are his last words before he dies. I mean, this guy's just amazing. Awesome. Mind-blowing. And I'm not the only one who thinks that.

There's this centurion, standing by the cross – hard-bitten sort of guy who's crucified more people than he'd ever like to remember. Well, he's seen the whole thing and he's well impressed. 'I don't care what anyone says,' he declares. 'This was a good guy!'

Well, it's all over – or so they think. The crowds begin to disperse. They're sorry now, of course – well, it's safe to be sorry now, when it's too late to do anything about it. Anyway, they all slope off, but his friends are still there – including the women who've been right behind him all the way from Galilee. They're just standing at a distance, watching everything. A kind of vigil.

Perhaps they think it's all over.

It isn't yet.

A passion for people

Crib sheet

Love story – but not a man-woman thing. Happy ending left until later – try and stay with the hope, today.

Jesus has been arrested – mob-handed – very courageous! Tried at High Priest's house, then dragged off to Pilate (they don't like him, just need him).

> Pilate's HQ – trumped up charges, lies/distortions: taxes . . . Messianic claims.
>
> Pilate: 'Are *you* a king?'
>
> Jesus: 'You're the one who's used the word.'

Leaders mention Galilee, so Pilate sends him to Herod, who mocks and sends him back in 'royal' robe.

Pilate: 'Flog and then release him' – rabble scream for Barabbas – Pilate gives in like a sensible politician!

Simon of Cyrene – Jesus' words to the women: weep for your children.

> Place of the skull – crucified between two rebels – prays for people's forgiveness – amazing!
>
> People gamble for his clothes – sign overhead.

Still something about him – rebels mock but one defends. Noon – darkness – curtain rent in two.

> Jesus' cry of faith – dies. Centurion's faith.

People disperse. Friends and women remain – vigil.

Perhaps they think it's all over – it isn't yet.

They think it's all over

Based on Luke 24:1-12

So, they think it's all over. Jesus' friends, that is. Fitted up, convicted – well, that's actually dignifying it a bit: his enemies got the rabble going and frightened the governor into sentencing him. Call it a trial? It wasn't even a respectable perversion of justice!

Anyway, that's it. It's now Sunday morning – and it's as if that strange, eerie darkness that came down at midday on Friday has never truly lifted. The whole world's dark now.

Still, the women think it's important to be faithful to him. There was no time for proper burial rites on Friday; yesterday was the Sabbath, and they couldn't work then – so today's the first chance to put that right. And here they are, at the very breaking of dawn, coming to the tomb where he was buried. They're carrying spices they've prepared, so that they can anoint his body.

Now, this really is weird: the tomb's open. It was sealed on Friday, but now it's wide open – the big stone that was rolled across the entrance now rests at the side of it, and there's this big, dark, yawning hole. I tell you, it's creepy. So, they're edging forward – probably huddled together, each hoping one of the others will look inside so they don't have to – when suddenly they've got company: two guys in dazzling, shining robes, and they're standing right beside them.

Now, this is *so* not what the women were expecting. I mean, the darkness was bad enough, but now it's getting scary. All they can do is look at the ground and hope the apparitions

They think it's all over

> will go away. No such luck – before they know what's happening, the guys are talking to them. 'What's this about?' they ask. Funny – that's exactly what the women would have asked *them* if their mouths hadn't been fully occupied in the gaping and gasping routine. 'Why are you looking for a living person where only the dead should be?' Well, that'd be a good question – except that the person they're looking for *is* dead – isn't he?

While the women are still trying to get their heads round it, the men continue. 'He's not here, you know – really, he's not. He's risen. Hey, don't you remember? He told you all about this while you were with him in Galilee: Son of Man, handed over to sinners – crucified – rising on the third day – remember now?'

That's when the penny drops – except that they've never heard of slot machines, but we'll let that pass – and they remember Jesus' words. So they don't hang around – they're off like lightning, back to the eleven and all the other friends of Jesus, to tell them the news.

> Now, remember there are quite a few witnesses here: Mary Magdalene, Joanna, Mary the mother of James, a few others – a good number. So, what do the guys think when they hear the story?

Rubbish.

'Old wives' tales' (what'll you bet that that was a phrase men invented too?).

So, there they are, with the greatest news the world's ever had – and no one's believing them.

Well, I'm not sure about 'no one' – where's Peter gone?

He's gone to the tomb – running like nothing else matters – and when he gets there he goes one stage further. He bends down and actually looks inside. Well, give him his due – he's a braver man than I am, whatever he might have got wrong in the past. He peers into the tomb – and there, lying on the ledge, in full view . . .

Linen grave-clothes – empty ones – just lying there. Now, it's obvious that this really gets to him because he just wanders off in a daze, to think about it.

So, what *has* happened?

Oh, I know it's all a bit low-key at the moment – but that's often how God works, isn't it?

I tell you, the world's in for the surprise of its entire existence.

Think it's all over?

It's only just beginning!

They think it's all over

Crib sheet

So, they think it's all over . . .

Now Sunday morning – dark – women coming with spices.

> Weird – tomb's open – scary!
>
> Two men in dazzling robes – women keep heads down.
>
> Men: 'Why search for the living among the dead? Not here – risen – just as he said.'

They remember!

Back to tell the eleven and other friends.

'Old wives' tale.'

> Peter runs to the tomb.
>
> Bends down – looks inside – sees empty grave-clothes.
>
> Wanders off in a daze.

All a bit low-key? That's how God often works, isn't it?

World's in for a surprise.

Think it's all over?

It's just beginning!

Don't just sit there – communicate

Based on Acts 2:1-11

Right – does anybody speak a foreign language?

(Business with audience.)

Of course, there's one foreign language you all speak, isn't there?

Intergalactic Esperanto.

What? No one speaks Intergalactic Esperanto?

So, let me get this straight. You're space-age people – at this very moment scientists are exploring far-flung galaxies with probes and telescopes – and you don't speak Intergalactic Esperanto. So, what are you going to do if you meet aliens?

It was a bit like that for Peter and his friends.

They weren't going on a spaceship – but they were in a town full of aliens. And they really had to communicate with them – urgently.

It all started with Jesus – you know the story – he gets killed – God raises him to new life again – Jesus goes back to heaven.

But before he goes, he gives them a little job to do. 'Tell people about me,' he says. Sounds simple enough – how many people did he want them to tell? Couple of dozen, maybe? A hundred? A thousand?

Only all the people in the world, that's all.

> Three thousand extra people, in one evening, speaking different languages and understanding each other perfectly.

That's the power of God's Spirit at work.

I mean, compared with that, Intergalactic Esperanto's a piece of cake.

Stories for telling

Crib sheet

Intergalactic Esperanto?

> It all started with Jesus – 'Tell everyone about me.'
> Oh, sure – all these different languages!

Festival – town's full of foreign visitors

So there they are:
- We're bored!
- When are we going to get started?
- We need decent leadership.

> Sound of wind.
> Flames – but not burning.
> Remember the burning bush?

Out into the street – not nervous any more!
- Peter speaking Turkish.
- Andrew and Persian carpet salesman.
- Thomas arguing with Greek professors.
- Philip using sign language.

> 3,000 people come to believe.
> That's the power of God's spirit at work.
> Intergalactic Esperanto? A piece of cake!